Jane + Robin

Great stuf

Enjoy

Candore Diane +
Hannah

The Secret to Tender Pie

The Secret to Tender Pie

America's Grandmothers Share
Their Favorite Recipes

Mindy Marin

BALLANTINE BOOKS * NEW YORK

http://www.randomhouse.com

Library of Congress Catalog Card Number: 97-93151

ISBN: 0-345-40985-X

BOOK DESIGN BY BTD / ROBIN BENTZ

Manufactured in the United States of America
First Edition: May 1997

10   9   8   7   6   5   4   3   2

For my grandma
Bessie Cecil

✴ *Contents* ✴

Bessie Cecil

* Preface *

The Secret to Tender Pie is a book inspired by my grandmother Bessie Cecil, and a recipe she gave to me. The idea came during the Christmas of '92 when my grandmother asked me what I wanted as a present. At that moment, I remembered the years of my childhood—watching her, at family gatherings, conducting her particular brand of magic that stirred so many of our delicious celebratory meals. Her children and their children—and soon, their children's children—taking part. Cooking aromas from her youth and what her very own mother taught her came wafting through the kitchen, year after year. Turkey and cranberry sauce, mashed potatoes laced with butter, smells of apples and cinnamon.

It struck me that what I really wanted was the recipe for her apple pie. Two weeks later I received a letter in the mail from my grandmother telling me one of her secrets: the Secret to Tender Pie. While reading her letter, it occurred to me that if my grandma has a recipe that means so much to me, so must grandmothers everywhere. Since ours has not been a culture that honors our elders, I felt I wanted to make a contribution toward changing how we view a generation that has so much to teach us. For the next two years I set out in search of recipes all over the country. I stopped women on airplanes, in market aisles, at family functions, on Sunday drives through Amish country in Pennsylvania. I hounded mothers and grandmothers of friends, sought out suspects at swap meets; wherever there was a grandma was where I hoped to be. I was shameless. The *Los Angeles Times* Food Section ran an article about my efforts, and before I knew it, there were hundreds of recipes from which to choose. After much laboring over which recipes and their authors best reflected the spirit of the book, it is now that I share with you not only a secret from my grandmother but secrets of grandmothers from all across America. It is a book of memories, of recipes and photographs that will bring you back to your grandma's childhood and to generations lived the world over.

*

Acknowledgments

I would like to thank my family: my mother, Jana, who will certainly be a grandmother one day; my father, John, and my brothers, Alden and Britt. Thanks to my soulmate, Douglas Mellor, who has stood by me on this journey. To my three aunts, Kathleen, Virginia, and Lois, who helped me corral the White Tornado. Hats off to Christopher Cerf, who introduced me to my wonderful editors at Ballantine, Peter Gethers and Amy Scheibe. My heartfelt gratitude to Peter and Amy, who believed from the beginning; Maura Wogan, who was in charge of not believing until it was in writing. Thank you to Robert Legg; John and Susie; Laurie Sawyer; Suzanne; Charles Perry from the *Los Angeles Times*; Janet Fletcher; Susan Fairbairn; Ira Schreck; Guy Webster; and Kismet, who was in charge of eating the crumbs. Thanks to my friends, The Tender Pie Tasters: Debbie Adelman and Joan Vogel from The Ojai Cook Culinary Center; Traci Donat and her husband, Lucas; Paige Peterson; Claudia Taylor; and the conductor of all cooks, Victoria Granof. To Sharon Owyang for her saving grace and good company, and to the rest of my friends, who shared in the excitement.

My deepest gratitude is to all of our grandmothers, who shared their wisdom by way of food. We honor you.

*

The Secret to Tender Pie

Bride's Biscuits

EVELYN MCIVER

2 cups flour
2½ teaspoons baking powder
1 teaspoon salt
4 tablespoons shortening, chilled, plus
   2 tablespoons for dipping tops
⅔ cup buttermilk

Preheat oven to 450°F. Sift the dry ingredients together; cut in shortening. Stir in the milk and beat with a spoon until blended. Knead on a floured board for a few minutes. Press down with hand until half-inch thick.

In oven, heat an 11 × 7-inch pan with a small amount of shortening until the shortening is melted. Cut the biscuits with a floured 2-inch round biscuit cutter and place in pan, turning once so that the tops have been dipped in shortening. It makes them golden crisp. Bake for 10 to 12 minutes, until golden brown.

received this recipe from my friend Virginia Grier at my bridal shower forty-one years ago. Her mother-in-law used to make these biscuits every morning. They are the best. Dipping them in the melted shortening and turning them over is the secret to a fine biscuit.

Evelyn McIver

WAS BORN ON AUGUST 31, 1932, IN BEEKLER, KANSAS. SHE HAS TWO CHILDREN AND ONE GRANDCHILD.

Mrs. Blair's Irish Soda Bread

MICHAEL LEARNED

4 cups flour

2 teaspoons salt

1½ teaspoons baking soda

¼ teaspoon baking powder

⅓ cup sugar

1 cup raisins

1½–1¾ cups buttermilk or sour cream

2 eggs

1 tablespoon melted butter, if desired,
   for tops

Preheat oven to 350°F. Sift the dry ingredients together. Stir in raisins. In a separate bowl, combine buttermilk and eggs. Add to the flour and raisin mixture, mixing only until moistened.

Form 2 round loaves. Bake for 45 minutes. Brush with butter as the bread bakes.

rs. Blair arrived dressed in a borrowed original Dior suit, white gloves, and a god-awful gray wig. I was about to go on tour and was desperate to find a suitable caretaker for my three young, very rambunctious sons and their assorted pets: guinea pigs; hamsters; our cat, Rosie; and daily accumulations of toads, snails, garter snakes, et al. My heart sank. She seemed so frail, so dignified. Could she cope? She sure could! For twelve years she loved and cared for us all. She was mother to me, grandmother to my sons, and overall angel from heaven. This is her recipe for Irish soda bread. It's great on a cold or rainy day; it makes you feel cozy and loved.

Michael Learned

WAS BORN ON APRIL 9, 1939, IN WASHINGTON, D.C. SHE HAS THREE CHILDREN AND THREE GRANDCHILDREN.

✳ *Banana Nut Bread* ✳

EDIE ANDREWS

1 cup sugar
¼ cup shortening
3 mashed ripe bananas
2 eggs, beaten
2 cups flour
1 teaspoon baking soda
½ cup chopped walnuts or pecans
    (optional)

    Preheat oven to 375°F. Grease and flour one 8″ × 4″ loaf pan. Set aside. Sift flour with baking soda. In a separate bowl, cream sugar and shortening until light. Add eggs to sugar mixture one at a time, beating well after each addition. Beat in mashed bananas, then flour mixture (on low speed if using an electric mixer). Fold in chopped nuts if desired. Pour into prepared loaf pan and bake at 375° for 40–45 minutes or until top springs back when lightly touched with finger. Allow to cool in pan for 10 minutes. Then turn out onto a rack to cool completely.

    Yield: one loaf

I never knew my grandmother. When I was growing up, my mother and sister worked, so I had to have supper ready every night when they came home. That's how I learned to cook. I've had this recipe for years on a worn-out index card. I've always baked the bread in a long, thin, greased pan (3½″ x 12″) at 350° for 55–60 minutes. The children liked it this way. You didn't have to do so much cutting and could spread butter all over. I still make this whenever I get a batch of old and soft bananas. The older the bananas, the easier they are to mash.

Edie Andrews

WAS BORN ON NOVEMBER 25, 1924, IN
WEST DENNIS, MASSACHUSETTS. SHE HAD
SIX CHILDREN (TWO ARE NOW DECEASED),
HAS SIX GRANDCHILDREN, AND THREE
GREAT-GRANDCHILDREN.

Lou Lee's Corn Bread

LOU LEE WILLIAMS

1 cup all-purpose flour
1 cup cornmeal (make it a good quality, fresh yellow meal)
3 teaspoons baking powder
1 teaspoon salt
¼ cup canola oil
1 egg
1 cup milk

Preheat oven to 450°F. Combine the flour, cornmeal, baking powder, and salt in a mixing bowl.

Preferably in a cast-iron skillet, heat the canola oil in the oven until it is sizzling hot (about 5 minutes). Meanwhile, beat together the egg and the milk

Add the egg mixture to the dry ingredients and—contrary to many corn bread recipes—give this batter a good little whippin' with a wooden spoon (a "gentle beating"). This brings out the gluten in the flour and gives the corn bread a more bread-like texture than usual. (Good for soppin'.) Add the hot oil to the corn bread batter all at once, mixing thoroughly.

Pour the batter into the skillet and return skillet to oven. Bake for about 25 minutes, or until golden brown.

This is great with collard greens and pot likker (the cooking juices from the greens) and also makes a fabulous dressing for fowl.

Note: The secret is in the mixing and this corn bread is meant for soppin'.

CORN BREAD DRESSING
Crumbled corn bread
1 cup finely chopped onion
1 cup finely chopped celery
4 tablespoons butter
2 teaspoons poultry seasoning, or to taste
Salt and pepper

Simply crumble the corn bread into a large mixing bowl. Sauté the chopped onion and celery in the butter. Add to the crumbled corn bread with fresh poultry seasoning to taste and salt and pepper. Fill cavity of bird. Truss and bake at 350°F. for 20 minutes per pound.

When I was a little girl, we had corn bread every day and it was my job to help make it. I remember big wedges, fresh and hot from the oven, slathered with freshly churned butter from our cows. The height of corn bread eating for me is with a nice bowl of collard greens served with scallions from our garden. We'd eat the greens and at the bottom of the bowl was the rich pot likker. I'd take the corn bread, crumble it with my fingers into the pot likker, and then eat it with my hands — it was sublime. That's the way to eat corn bread.

Lou Lee Williams

WAS BORN ON MAY 5, 1918, IN MARLTON, ARKANSAS. SHE HAS SIX CHILDREN AND TWELVE GRANDCHILDREN.

✳ *Grandma Della's Challa* ✳

CAROLE R. BROWENDER

1 package active dry yeast
1¼ cups warm water
1½ teaspoons salt
¼ cup sugar
¼ cup vegetable oil
2 eggs
5–5½ cups unbleached all-purpose flour

FOR THE GLAZE:
1 egg yolk, beaten with 1 teaspoon water
Sesame or poppy seeds, optional

In a large bowl, dissolve the yeast in the water. Stir in the salt, sugar, oil, and eggs. With an electric mixer, gradually beat in approximately 4½ cups of the flour to make a stiff dough. Attach the dough hook to the mixer and add more flour, ½ cup at a time, until the mixture forms a smooth, satiny dough. Knead, either by hand or by machine, for 5 to 20 minutes, until the dough is smooth and elastic, adding small amounts of flour as needed to prevent sticking.

Place the dough in a greased bowl, turning to grease top. Cover and let rise in a warm place until doubled in bulk (about 1½ hours).

Grease 1 cookie sheet or 2 bread pans. Punch down dough. Divide into 6 equal pai

Roll each part into a rope 10 to 12 inches long. Braid 3 ropes together for each loaf and place on cookie sheet. Cover and let rise until doubled (45 minutes to 1 hour).

Preheat oven to 350°F. Brush the tops of both loaves with the egg mixture and sprinkle with seeds if desired. Bake for 30 to 35 minutes, until golden brown.

Note: I often make this recipe into 6 small loaves by using greased mini-loaf pans and dividing dough, after first rising, into 6 pieces, and each of those pieces into thirds.

My grandma Della Weitzman was a tiny (not quite five feet tall), feisty, energetic woman, a fabulous cook who kept all her recipes in her head because she was never taught to read and write. She died at 102 years of age, but her recipes and sayings live on. When she was asked for the recipe for something, her measurements were ge-sheterra (Yiddish for "a dash of this and a pinch of that until it feels right").

After the death of my grandfather, Grandma Della went to live with her youngest daughter, Sylvia. Sylvia's mission in life was to try and preserve these marvelous ethnic recipes, so she measured everything as Grandma cooked. In turn I got these recipes from Aunt Sylvia. My children all fondly remember their grandma Della and her delicious food and say that my efforts are almost as good as Grandma Della's.

Carole Browender
(bride)

WAS BORN ON MAY 16, 1933,
IN MILWAUKEE, WISCONSIN. SHE
HAS THREE CHILDREN AND
FOUR GRANDCHILDREN.

✳ *Apple Cider French Toast* ✳

IDA MAE CASH MCQUADE

FOR THE FRENCH TOAST:

6 eggs

½ cup sugar

1 teaspoon vanilla

1 cup milk

1 loaf (about 1 pound) challah or other
    unsliced bread (see Grandma Della's
    Challa, page 10)

Apple pie filling

¼ cup butter

FOR THE SYRUP:

½ gallon apple cider

2 cinnamon sticks

Preheat oven to 400°F. Beat together the eggs, sugar, vanilla, and milk. Cut the challah into 1½-inch slices and slit each slice along the crust to form a pocket. Add a spoonful of apple pie filling and soak for a few minutes in batter. This would be a good use for an extra half batch of Grandma Bessie's Apple Pie Filling (see page 92), cooked without the crust in an 8 × 8-inch baking dish for 45 minutes, covered, at 375°F.

Melt the butter in a jelly roll pan. Add the slices of battered bread and bake for 15 minutes.

To make the syrup: Boil the apple cider with the cinnamon sticks down to a rich consistency.

Serve the French toast with the syrup. Add ¼ cup quince jelly to the syrup *after* reducing the heat and let cool to warm temperature. This will help thicken the syrup and add some "spice." Makes this special and easier than apple pie.

I met my husband in high school. We soon started traveling around the world as a second-generation military family. I opened a bed-and-breakfast, The Chatelaine, in Pine Grove Mills, Pennsylvania. I have always loved to cook and entertain.

I never thought that running a bed-and-breakfast would be my forte. Dinner parties are so much easier. The guests don't come until evening and they leave after the meal. Breakfast for a pay-ing crowd is a different matter. It must be early, delicious, and beautiful. I developed this French toast recipe for my bed-and-breakfast. I love doing it because I can do it in one fell swoop for eight.

Now Shaun, Simon, and Alex get to eat Apple Cider French Toast when they visit from Oklahoma and Nebraska, miles and miles from Pennsylva-nia but close to their grandmother's heart.

Ida Mae Cash McQuade

WAS BORN ON SEPTEMBER 25, 1928, IN RISON, ARKANSAS. SHE HAS FOUR CHILDREN AND THREE GRANDCHILDREN.

✳ *Papoo's Pancakes* ✳

KATHLEEN KEATING

FOR THE PANCAKES:

2 eggs
1 cup flour
½ teaspoon baking powder
1 scant teaspoon salt
2 cups milk
½ cup melted butter
Oil for greasing griddle (approximately
    2 tablespoons)

FOR THE SAUCE:

½ cup butter
1 cup maple syrup
1 cup brown sugar
2 tablespoons water

First, prepare the sauce, and simmer the
ingredients together.

Beat the eggs until they are lemon color.
Add the dry ingredients alternately with the
milk and melted butter.

Bake thin, plate-size pancakes one at a time
on a greased griddle or large frying pan over
medium-high heat, turning when bubbly and
dry on surface. Turn only once. Stack on a
large plate in a warm oven. Every third cake,
drizzle syrup. To serve, cut the stack in
wedges and pass extra sauce.

✳

The recipe is really from my father. He had pancakes like this in the 1890s, when he was a child, and called them French Pancakes. I had them in the 1920s growing up with an older brother and twin sister. My children, two boys and two girls, had them at special-occasion Sunday breakfasts in the 1940s. Now my seven grandsons and four granddaughters have them on special holidays. Papa died in 1976, but some of my older grandchildren remember him. And so we call the recipe Papoo's Pancakes.

Kathleen Keating

WAS BORN ON JULY 19, 1916,
IN LINCOLN, NEBRASKA. SHE HAS
FOUR CHILDREN AND ELEVEN
GRANDCHILDREN.

Apfelküchle (Small Apple Cake) ✶

HENRIETTA HARTMANN

4 eggs, separated
4 tablespoons sugar
1 teaspoon baking powder
1 teaspoon salt
1 teaspoon vanilla
4 tablespoons melted butter (tastes good,
    but it's optional)
1 cup flour
¾ cup milk (scant)
2 cups chunky applesauce

Grease griddle with melted butter or shortening. Begin to heat. Beat the egg yolks; add
the sugar, baking powder, salt, vanilla, and
melted butter. Mix well. Whisk in flour and
milk alternately. Mix in the applesauce, then
gently fold in the stiffly beaten egg whites.

Cook on hot griddle, turning once, until
browned.

Serve with butter and cinnamon sugar.
(Don't let anyone talk you into syrup.) For a
special breakfast, serve with fresh fruit cut up
and drizzled with champagne.

Yield: 4 servings

Note: To increase, go by ¼ recipe per
person.

✶

I was born in 1921 at my parents' house on Hayworth Avenue in Hollywood. I still remember with delight frolicking in the red sea of poinsettia fields belonging to my uncle, the legendary grower Paul Eche. But my fondest memory is of gathering around the kitchen table on Sunday mornings and holidays for Auntie Magdalena's Apfelküchle. The tradition continues. Family get-togethers happen at the drop of a hat with the lure of this Swiss treat, a family treasure for decades. The contemporary addition of mimosas only adds to the festivity.

Henrietta Hartmann

WAS BORN ON MAY 19, 1921, IN HOLLYWOOD, CALIFORNIA. SHE HAS FOUR CHILDREN AND THREE GRANDCHILDREN.

✳ *Cheese Blintzes* ✳

MANDY EINSTEIN

FOR THE CREPES:

1 cup flour
1 teaspoon salt
1 cup milk
4 eggs, well beaten
Butter for pan

FOR THE FILLING:

16 ounces hoop cheese
3 eggs
Salt, a pinch
½ cup sugar (or less if desired)
Cinnamon, a pinch

To make the crepes: Add the flour, salt, and milk to beaten eggs and beat again. Make crepes, using an 8-inch pan and cooking only one side until lightly cooked. Turn each crepe onto wax paper until all the crepes are cooked.

To make the filling: Beat all the ingredients together, but leave the mixture lumpy and thick. Place a generous tablespoon of filling on the cooked side of a crepe and fold the bottom up partway over the filling; then fold both sides to the middle and fold over again toward the top, completely enclosing the filling. Continue until all the crepes are filled. (At this point you can cover them with plastic wrap and refrigerate for several hours.)

To cook: Melt a little butter in a pan, add the crepes, and cook until golden brown.

Serve warm with a dollop of sour cream and sprinkle a combination of sugar and a little cinnamon mixed together. You can also serve them with sour cream and preserves or fresh fruit, but our favorite was the sugar-and-cinnamon combination.

✳

This was my mom's recipe that I've used and passed on to my children. When my parents moved from Chicago to Los Angeles in 1944, my mom said the blintzes always reminded her of home and made the move to a new city easier. This recipe is filled with love and fond memories of making blintzes with my mom, and then with my daughter.

Mandy Einstein

WAS BORN ON MAY 3, 1941, IN CHICAGO, ILLINOIS. SHE HAS TWO CHILDREN AND ONE GRANDCHILD.

✳ *Grandma Doughnuts* ✳

ALYCE THORN

7½ cups flour
1 teaspoon nutmeg
8 teaspoons baking powder
2 teaspoons salt
2 cups sugar
10 tablespoons butter, chilled
6 eggs, lightly beaten
2 cups milk
Grease or shortening for deep-frying

    Mix all dry ingredients. Cut in chilled butter until the texture is like cornmeal. Add eggs and milk and stir till dough comes together. Wrap in plastic. Chill for 2 hours.

    Heat grease to 375°F. Roll out dough to ½-inch thickness and cut with doughnut cutter. Deep-fry. Drain on paper towels.

When I was two, my four sisters and brothers came to live with our grandparents on a small farm north of Bagley, Minnesota. My grandma Nee had very bad arthritis, but the pain didn't stop her from teaching all of us how to make good doughnuts. She said: "Be sure your shortening is always hot"—at that time she used lard rendered from the butchered pigs—"and it's important not to overload the fryer or pan. Only fry two or three doughnuts at a time to keep the temperature from dropping. Drain the doughnuts well on brown paper bags." (She didn't have paper towels in those days.)

Grandma Doughnuts—that's what my great-grandchildren call their favorite doughnuts. When my grandchildren come to visit, it is an automatic given that they will be taking home a package of doughnuts. This does not leave many for my children, so at times they have to ask me to make a special batch for them.

Alyce Thorn

WAS BORN ON SEPTEMBER 16, 1914, IN ADMIRAL SACK, CANADA. SHE HAS THREE CHILDREN, ELEVEN GRANDCHILDREN, AND EIGHT GREAT-GRANDCHILDREN.

Artichoke Soup

DALLAS PRICE

6 large artichokes
1 bay leaf
3 whole cloves
3 peppercorns
1 teaspoon salt
1 sliced onion
1 tablespoon butter
1 quart chicken broth
Reserved artichoke liquid
1 cup whipping cream
Dash of nutmeg
$\frac{1}{8}$ teaspoon pepper

FOR THE CROUTONS:
Sourdough bread, cubed
Olive oil
Dash of garlic salt

Stand artichokes in a big pan in about 1 inch of water. Add bay leaf, cloves, and 1 teaspoon peppercorns. Add 1 teaspoon salt. Cook the artichokes over medium heat 40 to 45 minutes, until the artichokes are soft and you can pierce them with a fork. Drain the artichokes, reserving the liquid. When the artichokes are cool, scrape the pulp off the leaves by hand. Take the stringy stuff off the heart and discard. Meanwhile, sauté onion in butter until softened but not brown. Combine with artichoke pulp and set aside.

Put a little of the pulp and chicken broth in a food processor and blend. Keep blending in small increments until all the pulp is gone and the mixture has a soupy consistency. If it starts to get too thick, you can add the artichoke liquid.

Blend cream and nutmeg into this mixture. You can make this soup ahead of time and freeze it. On the morning of Christmas Eve, I thaw the soup and serve it in a big tureen with croutons.

To make the croutons, cube the sourdough bread. You can keep or discard the crust, to suit your preference. Cover the bottom of a huge frying pan with olive oil. Sprinkle the bottom with a little garlic salt. Turn each cubed bread piece over and over until it is evenly toasted.

Sprinkle croutons at the last minute so they don't become mushy.

T his is my traditional Christmas Eve dinner soup. I serve it with fresh croutons, fresh cracked Dungeness crab in a mustard sauce, and melted brie smothered in slivered almonds. For this festive event, I use twenty-four artichokes, each of them lovingly shaped by hand.

Dallas Price

WAS BORN ON FEBRUARY 2, 1933, IN PASADENA, CALIFORNIA. SHE HAS FIVE CHILDREN AND EIGHT GRANDCHILDREN.

✳ *Modeane's Kwanzaa Bean Soup* ✳

MODEANE NICHOLS THOMPSON

1 pint assorted dried beans
Salt
1 ham hock or 2 bouillon cubes
4 to 5 cups of water plus additional for
    soaking
1 can (16 ounces) crushed tomatoes,
    with juice
1 tablespoon Worcestershire sauce
¼ cup red or white wine, optional

THE SECRET SEASONINGS:
1 large clove garlic
1 tablespoon chili powder
1 teaspoon cumin
¼ teaspoon filé powder, optional
1 teaspoon thyme
½ teaspoon rosemary leaves, crushed

Soak the beans overnight. Rinse, drain. Salt to taste. Add the secret seasonings and ham hock. Cover with 4 to 5 cups of water and bring to a boil. Turn heat to low. Cover; simmer 1 to 2 hours, or until tender, stirring occasionally.

Add the crushed tomatoes and juice. Bring back to simmer. Reduce heat; cook uncovered 15 to 20 minutes more. Stir in the Worcestershire sauce and, if you feel adventuresome, the wine.

Warms hearts on a cold day.
Serves: **8–10**

Note: Filé powder is made from dried sassafras leaves and is essential for thickening a traditional gumbo. It gives a delicate flavor similar to that of thyme but must be used sparingly. Do not allow a gumbo to boil after adding filé, as it will become stringy. Actually, this may be where the word *filé* came from, as it is derived from the French word for "thread."

✳

For the last thirty years, my husband and I have entertained old and new friends at a "noninvitational" New Year's Day Open House. It's a standing invitation, and old friends and new acquaintances from all over drop in. The main menu includes, in addition to the usual holiday goodies, the old Southern traditional dishes of black-eyed peas and collard greens for good luck.

My special good luck gift for Open House guests is a container of my famous Kwanzaa Bean Soup Mix, a mixture of twelve to fifteen different kinds of dried beans and a secret blend of seasonings, with the printed recipe on the container. That's a gift which, I've been told, is used for "snow days," or simply to perk up a tired winter palate or to brighten up a kitchen shelf. For several friends, they've become collector's items, to be used only in emergencies.

Modeane Nichols Thompson

WAS BORN ON MARCH 28, 1929, IN MEMPHIS, TENNESSEE. SHE HAS FIVE CHILDREN AND SEVEN GRANDCHILDREN.

✳ Ruby Begonia's Chicken and Dumpling Soup ✳

R U B Y   K I N N

FOR THE SOUP:

**16 cups water plus additional for cooking
  dumplings**
1 whole chicken with skin
1 whole onion, peeled
**5 stalks celery, chopped in ¼-inch pieces
  (save the leaves)**
**1 teaspoon pickling spices (put them in wire
  tea ball and float in soup)**
7 chicken bouillon cubes (Knorr)
2 tablespoons olive oil
1 tablespoon butter
6 carrots, peeled and cut into small rounds
1 bay leaf

FOR THE DUMPLINGS:

3 cups flour
12 eggs
¼–½ cup beer
Salt and pepper

Fill a large soup pot with the 16 cups of water. Add the whole chicken with skin. Add the whole onion, washed celery leaves, pickling spices, and bouillon cubes. Bring to a boil, then simmer until the chicken is thoroughly cooked. When the chicken is cooked, take it out and remove the skin. Pull the chicken meat off the bones and return it to the pot.

While the chicken is cooking, heat the olive oil over medium-high heat in a pot large enough to accommodate the vegetables. Melt the butter. Add the celery pieces and the cut carrots. Sauté until tender, stirring frequently. When the vegetables are tender, put them in the soup pot.

To make the dumplings: In a large mixing bowl, combine the flour, eggs, beer, and salt and pepper. You want the batter to be just runny enough to drop off your spoon (slightly thicker than pancake batter). You drop this mixture one tablespoonful at a time into 3 inches of boiling water, to which a bouillon cube has been added for taste. Boil until firm (approximately 10 to 12 minutes), taking out dumplings and putting them into the soup pot as you go along. There may be leftover dumplings. Freeze and save to add to the soup later.

Bring the soup to a boil and boil for 15 minutes. Turn heat to low and simmer with the lid partially on while you cook the dumplings in a separate pot. This soup gets better with age.

✳

I was born Ruby Ellen Harrington on the sixth of July 1927. My father always used to say how grateful he was I hadn't been born on the Fourth because then I'd really be a firecracker! I was the only girl in a family of five children and I was definitely the black sheep. I rode a Harley-Davidson, and during the war my best friend, Rosie, and I were riveters. We made bayonet mounts for rifles in an army munitions plant.

This soup recipe has been around almost as long as I can remember. It was one of the first things I inherited from my mother-in-law after I married my husband in 1946. It is a Ukrainian recipe passed down for many generations. The men in the family used to joke that it was "Polish Penicillin." In my recollection no one who tasted it has ever had just one bowl.

Ruby Kinn

WAS BORN ON JULY 6, 1927, IN
PEQUOT LAKES, MINNESOTA. SHE HAS FIVE
CHILDREN, FOURTEEN GRANDCHILDREN,
AND TWO GREAT-GRANDCHILDREN.

✳ *Shrimp Gumbo* ✳

MYRTIS JUNE (GOFF) GOOCH

4 cups chopped tomatoes
1 pound okra, sliced
1 gallon water
1 cup cooking oil (or bacon grease,
    which is best)
½ cup flour
1 medium onion, chopped
5 tablespoons filé powder
2 pounds medium-size shrimp,
    peeled and deveined
1 cup crabmeat
Salt and pepper
1 tablespoon Tabasco

In large cooker, boil the tomatoes and okra
in the gallon of water on medium heat. In a
skillet, brown the oil and flour on medium-
low heat to make a roux. Add the chopped
onion to the roux and cook until the onion is
translucent. Add the roux to the tomatoes and
okra. Add filé powder and bring to a boil. Add
the shrimp and crab and continue to cook just
until the shrimp turns pink. Add salt, pepper,
and Tabasco to taste.

Serve over rice.

We were raised on the Gulf Coast of South Alabama. Seafood was a large part of our menu. Shrimp Gumbo was our favorite. After each marriage one of us would move to a different part of the South, but we remained a close-knit family. When one sibling could make it back home, the others would arrange to come back also, resulting in many homecomings. The last day of our visits, our mom would always fix her specialty, Shrimp Gumbo, which she was well known for. The recipe has been used many times since, but the result has never come up to hers. We have all concluded that the "secret" ingredient she used to make hers so special was Love.

Myrtis Gooch

WAS BORN MYRTIS JUNE GOFF
ON HER PARENTS' FARM IN PASCAGOULA,
MISSISSIPPI, ON DECEMBER 10, 1925.
SHE HAS THREE CHILDREN, FIVE
GRANDCHILDREN, AND FOUR
GREAT-GRANDCHILDREN.

Pedernales River Chili

CLAUDIA TAYLOR JOHNSON

4 pounds chili meat (coarsely ground
   round steak or well-trimmed chuck)
1 large onion, chopped
2 cloves garlic
1 teaspoon dried oregano
1 teaspoon comino seed (cumin)
6 teaspoons chili powder, or more if desired
1½ cups canned whole tomatoes
Hot pepper sauce, 2–6 generous dashes
Salt to taste
2 cups hot water

Put the meat, onion, and garlic in large,
heavy fry pan or Dutch oven. Cook until
light-colored. Add the oregano, comino seed,
chili powder, tomatoes, hot pepper sauce, salt
to taste, and hot water. Bring to a boil, lower
heat, and simmer for about 1 hour. Skim off
fat during cooking.

Lyndon always loved being at the ranch on the Pedernales River, and one of the reasons was the food. The ranch staff always knew to have plenty of things on hand that he liked because he often popped into the kitchen, sometimes alone, but more often with friends or strangers. One of his favorites was Pedernales River Chili, which he could never get enough of.

Claudia Taylor Johnson
(Lady Bird Johnson)

WAS BORN ON DECEMBER 22, 1912, IN KARNACK, TEXAS. SHE HAS TWO CHILDREN, SEVEN GRANDCHILDREN, AND TWO GREAT-GRANDCHILDREN.

Arroz Frito (Fried Rice)

MARINA RAMIREZ

6 tablespoons oil
½ cup finely chopped white onion
1 tomato, finely chopped
¼ green bell pepper, finely chopped
3 cups rice, washed and drained
6 cups water
3 teaspoons salt

Heat the oil in a large pot and add the onion, tomato, and bell pepper. Cook until the onion is translucent, 3 to 4 minutes. Add the rice and fry until the oil is completely absorbed and the rice is well mixed with vegetables, 3 to 4 minutes.

Add the water and salt, then cook on high heat until almost all the water is absorbed, about 10 minutes. Reduce heat to low, cover and cook 5 minutes more.

Note: Stir only once.

Yield: **6–8 servings.**

This recipe came from my mother. When I was growing up in San Salvador, my parents were away all day working and selling food far and wide. As the oldest child, I ended up raising my five younger siblings. I would often cook this dish for them. When cooking it, do not stir the rice more than once. Also be sure that the onion, tomatoes, and bell peppers are well cooked.

I came to the United States in 1985. Today, I still cook this dish for my family. My grandchildren consider their abuelita's rice their favorite dish!

Marina Ramirez

WAS BORN ON AUGUST 7, 1946, IN SAN SALVADOR, EL SALVADOR. SHE HAS FIVE CHILDREN AND FOUR GRANDCHILDREN.

Giambotta (Vegetable Mixture)

CONCETTA RINALDI

1 medium onion, sliced thin
1 clove of garlic, sliced thin
1 can (28 ounces) plum tomatoes, with juice
3 medium-size zucchini, sliced 2 inches
    thick and halved
3 medium-size Red Bliss potatoes, peeled
    and quartered
1 teaspoon oregano
Red pepper flakes
Salt and pepper to taste
6 leaves fresh basil or ½ teaspoon dried
2 eggs, beaten, optional

Sauté onion and garlic on medium heat until just golden. Do not brown. Chop the tomatoes coarsely and add with their juice. Simmer for 5 minutes. Add the zucchini, potatoes, oregano, a dash of red pepper flakes, and salt and pepper to taste. (Dried basil may be added with the other seasonings, but fresh basil should be added separately, just before serving, to maintain flavor.)

Simmer until fork-tender. When most of the juices have evaporated, add the beaten eggs and let set.

Serve with crusty bread or over a bed of farfalle (pasta shaped like butterflies or bow ties). A sprinkling of fresh, grated Parmesan would make a delicious addition at the end.

My mother, who was from Sicily, used to make Giambotta all the time. It brings back warm memories of my mother and all the cooking things she used to do. The children and grandchildren love it.

Concetta Rinaldi

WAS BORN ON DECEMBER 18, 1918, IN NEW YORK CITY. SHE HAS FIVE CHILDREN AND EIGHT GRANDCHILDREN.

✳ *Gram's Soul Stew* ✳

ANDREA MEAD LAWRENCE

1 pound lentils
4 or 5 carrots
5 good stalks of celery
2 large onions, or 10 pearl onions
1 clove garlic
2 or 3 bay leaves
2–4 ham hocks, optional
6 cups of water, plus additional as needed
2 cans (size 2½ or 28 ounces) tomatoes
    with juice
1 tablespoon parsley, chopped
Salt and pepper

POSSIBLE ADDITIONS INCLUDE:

Sausage
Hot dogs
Chicken thighs
Tofu (for total vegetarian)
Corn

Wash and rinse the lentils. Place the lentils in a large soup pot. Bring to a rapid boil in approximately 2 inches of water and boil for 2 minutes. Remove pot from fire for 1 hour while preparing vegetables and other ingredients.

Slice the carrots and celery, crush the garlic, quarter the onions. When ready to cook, add the garlic, bay leaves, ham hocks (if using them), and the 6 cups of water to the pot with the lentils. Bring to a boil. Reduce the heat and simmer, making sure when fluid is absorbed to add water so that the lentils are always covered. Follow this procedure twice and check for tenderness. Add tomatoes with their liquid (cut them up a little after adding), celery, onions, carrots, and parsley. Brew according to tenderness and aroma. Salt and pepper to taste. Now, add those "possible additions" if desired. Stew until it tastes and smells *good*!

✳

*S*ome secrets of mine for this dish: After cooking, set it aside and refrigerate overnight. It is better yet the second day, and it may be brewed with a good wine when cooking. This also goes well with a yummy, warm, homemade corn bread. [See Lou Lee's Corn Bread, page 8.] The key to a successful lentil stew is to customize it to taste. This is a recipe that I got from my mother back in the green hills of Vermont when we were all growing up at Pico Peak Ski Area, which my family developed in the mid-1930s.

Andrea Mead Lawrence

WAS BORN ON APRIL 19, 1932, IN RUTLAND, VERMONT. SHE HAS FIVE CHILDREN AND FOUR GRANDCHILDREN.

✳ *Wild Onion and Eggs* ✳

MAGGIE STUDIE

4 handfuls of wild onions
1½ cups water
Salt
3 tablespoons bacon grease or oil
4 eggs

    Gather wild onions early in spring. Clean the onions and cut off the roots. Chop into 1-inch lengths. Place in skillet along with the water. Add salt to taste. Cover and simmer about 10 minutes. Uncover and drain water.

    Add the bacon grease and raise temperature to medium high. Fry for 15 minutes at a lower temperature and add the eggs. Cook and stir until eggs are done.

This was my mom's recipe. Since I can remember, we have always eaten wild onions. We get wild onions in the woods; it's a special spring food in Oklahoma. I never miss eating it, even to this day.

Maggie Studie

WAS BORN ON APRIL 19, 1929, IN WELLING,
OKLAHOMA. SHE HAD FOUR CHILDREN
(ONE IS NOW DECEASED), AND HAS
EIGHT GRANDCHILDREN.

✳ *Crab and Shrimp Casserole* ✳

BEATRICE WESSON

½ **pound fresh mushrooms**
3 tablespoons butter plus 1 tablespoon
   for topping
1 pound crabmeat, cooked
1 pound medium-size shrimp, cooked
Paprika
½ **cup bread crumbs**

FOR THE SAUCE:
2 tablespoons butter
2 tablespoons flour
Hot sauce, optional
½ **cup milk**
½ **cup white wine**
½ **teaspoon dry mustard**
1 teaspoon dry tarragon
Salt and pepper

Preheat oven to 350°F. Sauté the mushrooms in the 3 tablespoons butter. Put the mushrooms, crab, and shrimp in a casserole.

Next make the sauce: Melt the 2 tablespoons of butter, then whisk in flour off the heat until smooth. Add the hot sauce with seasonings, if using. Slowly add the milk, wine, and remaining seasonings for the sauce while continuing to whisk. Cook the sauce for 2 to 3 minutes, then add it to the casserole.

Melt the remaining 1 tablespoon butter and mix into the bread crumbs. Sprinkle the bread crumbs on top of the casserole. Sprinkle with a dash of paprika. Bake uncovered for 30 minutes. Cover before serving.

✳

I got this recipe from my mother many many years ago when I was growing up in Louisiana. When she cooked, she never measured her ingredients and always went by feel. Through the years, I've made it a point to remember this recipe for Crab and Shrimp Casserole, which was a favorite of mine. I still make it nowadays. Everyone seems to love it.

Bea Wesson

WAS BORN ON OCTOBER 23, 1914, IN COLUMBIA, LOUISIANA. SHE HAS TWO SURVIVING CHILDREN (TWO OTHERS ARE DECEASED), TWELVE GRANDCHILDREN, FIVE GREAT-GRANDCHILDREN, AND THREE GREAT-GREAT-GRANDCHILDREN.

✳ *Shrimp Oreganato* ✳

MARY ELLEN DICOCCO

½ cup seasoned bread crumbs
6 teaspoons dried oregano
Salt and pepper
Crushed red pepper
1 tablespoon butter
1 tablespoon oil
1 large clove garlic, minced
1 pound shrimp
1 bottle (24 ounces) clam juice
½ cup chopped parsley

Combine the bread crumbs with the oregano, a dash of salt and pepper, and crushed red pepper to taste. In a sauté pan, melt the butter in the oil over medium-high heat, and when sizzling, add the garlic and shrimp. Cook until shrimp begin to turn pink.

Lower heat to medium. Begin to sprinkle the shrimp with the bread crumb mixture and stir, adding clam juice alternately with crumbs until the desired consistency is achieved. Sprinkle with parsley before serving.

Serve as an appetizer, with lots of Italian bread for dunking, or over linguine.

✳

My mother was a Russian immigrant and my father was French and English. In 1946 I married a wonderful Italian gentleman named Paul DiCocco, who was in the restaurant business. This recipe was obtained from a famous Italian chef who cooked at Anthony's Restaurant in Schenectady, New York. It has become a favorite among my children and grandchildren.

Mary Ellen DiCocco

WAS BORN MARY ELLEN BATES ON
AUGUST 28, 1928, IN SCHENECTADY,
NEW YORK. SHE HAS SIX CHILDREN AND
ELEVEN GRANDCHILDREN.

✴ *"Garfish" Stew* ✴

VERITIES JACOBS

4 fillets (6 ounces each) catfish, redfish,
    or garfish
1 teaspoon salt
½ teaspoon freshly ground black pepper
1 teaspoon garlic powder
1 teaspoon onion powder
½ cup plus 1 tablespoon flour
Oil for panfrying
4 chopped tomatoes, or 1 can (16 ounces)
    stewed tomatoes
6 stalks green onion
2 bay leaves, optional
1 rib celery, sliced
1 red bell pepper
1 green bell pepper
¼ teaspoon cayenne, optional

Season the fish fillets with salt, pepper, and onion and garlic powder. Dredge the fish fillets in ½ cup flour. Heat oil in a large skillet. Panfry the fillets until brown on both sides.

Remove the fillets and drain excess oil, leaving 1 tablespoonful in skillet. Whisk in the 1 tablespoon flour, making a roux. Continue to cook over medium-high heat until lightly brown. Return the fillets to the skillet. Add the tomatoes, green onions, bay leaves, celery, and red and green bell peppers, and let simmer for 10 to 15 minutes, or until vegetables are soft and gravy thickens.

Serve over rice.

Garfish is available in November in certain sections of the country. When unavailable, use catfish or redfish.

✴

My papa was a sharecropper, so me and my three sisters were raised off the land. My mama kept a small garden and was a very creative cook. Some of the dishes she would cook were baked possum and sweet potatoes, fried quail, hoecakes, hopping John (black-eyed peas and rice), smothered rabbit, squirrel dumplings, chicken dumplings, and all kinds of vegetables and desserts. One of my favorites was her fish stew.

Verities Jacobs

WAS BORN ON OCTOBER 25, 1917, IN GRAND CAPE, LOUISIANA. SHE HAS TWO CHILDREN, FIVE GRANDCHILDREN, AND NINE GREAT-GRANDCHILDREN.

✳ *Grandma B's Chicken* ✳

ANTOINETTE B. LIPPERT

1 chicken (pieces or quartered)
3 tablespoons olive oil
½ cup sliced onions
½ cup fresh or canned mushrooms
2 beef bouillon cubes
1 cup water
3 tablespoons sugar
2 teaspoons chopped parsley
2 teaspoons basil
¾ teaspoon oregano
Salt and pepper
1 can (48 ounces) tomato juice
½ cup dry white wine

Preheat oven to 375°F. Place the chicken in an open casserole or a small roasting pan (3-quart size) and brown for 40 minutes (turn over after the first 20 minutes).

While the chicken is browning, make Grandma B's special sauce. In a large skillet moistened with olive oil, brown the onions and mushrooms for 5 minutes on low heat. Dissolve the bouillon cubes in the water and add to the vegetables. Now add the sugar and herbs and a dash of salt and pepper and stir well. Then add the tomato juice and wine. Cover and simmer for 25 minutes.

Pour the sauce over the browned chicken and cook for another 30 minutes.

Serve with rice, Italian garden salad with red wine vinegar and olive oil dressing, and plenty of good crusty bread to dip in the sauce.

✳

When Grandma B's Chicken is cooking in my kitchen, it evokes precious memories of my mother trying to teach me how to cook as I approached "the marrying age." She would entreat me to sit in the kitchen and learn each step of the recipe. She wanted me to watch her pluck some remaining feathers off the chicken, then clean and cut it up. But I couldn't bear this tedious phase, so I said, "Mama, by the time I get married, they will sell chickens already plucked, cleaned, and cut up, so don't worry!" Fortunately, I was right about ready-to-cook chickens, but she was wiser when she made me learn how to cook this great Italian recipe.

This dish is also special to me because it was a favorite of my late son, Patrick. On his visits home from California, he would walk into the kitchen, sniff, and say, "Now I'm really home." This is the first recipe my mother taught to the new daughters-in-law in my family. It is still a favorite with Grandma B's third generation!

Antoinette B. Lippert

WAS BORN ON JANUARY 21, 1925, IN CHICAGO, ILLINOIS. SHE HAD SIX CHILDREN (ONE IS NOW DECEASED) AND EIGHT GRANDCHILDREN.

✳ *Nettie Tilton's Fried Chicken* ✳

MARTHA TILTON

1 frying chicken, cut up into serving pieces
1½ cups buttermilk
Flour
Salt and pepper
1 teaspoon dried parsley
1 teaspoon poultry seasoning
1 teaspoon dry mustard
Lard, canola oil, or butter (your choice)

Soak the chicken in the buttermilk for 30 minutes. Remove but do not dry the pieces. In a large Ziploc bag mix the flour, salt, pepper, parsley, poultry seasoning, and mustard. Shake the chicken pieces in bag with mixture.

Fry the chicken pieces until golden brown. Make sure you use plenty of oil.

My grandmother went to the chicken yard, did the young pullets in by wringing their necks, then removed the feathers after dipping the chicken in a pail of hot water. A lot of work, but we only had chicken on Sundays. Women in those days were certainly not sissies! I got this recipe from my mother, Nettie Tilton.

Martha Tilton

WAS BORN ON NOVEMBER 14, 1915, IN CORPUS CHRISTI, TEXAS. SHE HAS THREE CHILDREN AND FIVE GRANDCHILDREN.

☀ *Tailgate Chicken* ☀

BONNIE HARVEY

Flour for dredging
6 pounds large chicken thighs
4 eggs, beaten, or egg substitute
3 cups cracker crumbs or cracker meal
Canola oil for frying
1 cup sugar
1 cup light soy sauce
½ cup sherry
2 garlic cloves, crushed
Cooking oil

Flour the chicken. Shake off excess. Dip the chicken pieces in egg, then in cracker crumbs.

Fry the chicken pieces in ½ inch hot oil until each side is golden brown. Remove and place on paper towels to drain.

Preheat oven to 300°F. Combine the sugar, soy sauce, sherry, and garlic in saucepan and cook over medium heat until sugar dissolves. Line a large cookie sheet with foil and spray with cooking oil spray. Dip the chicken pieces in the sauce, one piece at a time, coating all sides thoroughly, then place them on the foil-lined cookie sheet. Bake for one hour, turning once during the process.

Note: For cracker crumbs, I use an 8-ounce box of saltine crackers, crushed.

☀

Bonnie Harvey

WAS BORN ON MAY 20, 1925, IN MERKEL,
TEXAS (A "SPOT IN THE ROAD" IN
WEST TEXAS). SHE HAD THREE CHILDREN
(ONE IS NOW DECEASED), AND HAS EIGHT
GRANDCHILDREN AND TWO STEP-
GRANDCHILDREN.

This recipe is great anytime, but is a favorite of my family as a tail-gate food at 49ers games because it can be served hot or cold. Now we can eat it at Oakland Raiders games too!

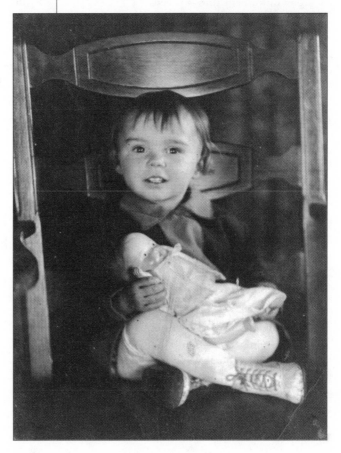

✳ *Madame Wong's Crispy Duck* ✳

MADAME WONG

1 duck (5 pounds)
2 tablespoons salt
1 piece gingerroot (¼-inch thick)
1 green onion, cut into 4 pieces
2 tablespoons dark soy sauce
6 tablespoons flour
2 quarts cooking oil
Plum sauce, optional

Wash the duck and wipe it dry. Rub with salt inside and out. Put gingerroot and green onion pieces inside the duck cavity and place the duck in the refrigerator for at least 4 hours.

Heat water to boiling in a steamer. Place the duck directly on the steamer tray. Steam, covered, for 1½ to 2 hours. Remove and allow to cool.

Brush the duck with soy sauce, then sprinkle it with flour, rubbing the flour well into the skin and coating thoroughly.

Heat the oil in a deep skillet, wok, or deep-fat fryer until it is very hot. Fry the duck until crisp and golden brown, turning occasionally, for about 15 minutes. Serve whole or cut into pieces, with plum sauce.

Yield: 4 servings

Crispy duck is a culinary favorite that is delicious with pea pods and mushrooms. Plain steamed buns and peppercorn salt are delicious accompaniments as well.

Note: A bamboo steamer is necessary for this dish. This recipe may be prepared in advance and refried before serving. It also may be frozen after the steaming. Plum sauce and bamboo steamers are available in most Asian grocery stores and many supermarkets.

✳

*C*ooking is life to me. Born into a family of twenty-two doctors, I am also the third generation in a family of cooks, following in the footsteps of my mother and grandmother. Growing up, I remember, it was my hobby to watch my mother cook. When I was in China, I taught cooking to consuls' wives from sixteen countries. In China, I taught Continental cuisine. In America, I teach Chinese cooking. When I came to this country in 1961, I had $1.25. America has treated me very well. All my cooking classes here have been fully attended. In the sixty years that I've been teaching cooking, there have been no criticisms. That is because I am very strict with myself. Whatever I do, I have to do well. And people appreciate that. To the Chinese, food is heaven.

S. T. Ting Wong

WAS BORN IN SHANGHAI, CHINA, ON THE
FOURTH DAY OF THE NINTH MOON IN THE
YEAR 4,603 (1905 BY THE WESTERN
CALENDAR). SHE HAD TWO CHILDREN
(NOW DECEASED), AND HAS
ONE GRANDCHILD.

✳ *Irish Stew* ✳

ALICE MCKECHNIE

3 pounds boneless leg of lamb cut into
   2″ chunks
½ cup carrots, peeled and cut into
   1″ chunks
½ cup turnip, peeled and cut into 1″ chunks
1 large onion, peeled and sliced ¼″ thick
4 cups potatoes, peeled and sliced ¼″ thick
¼ cup flour
¼ cup cold water
Salt and pepper to taste

Put lamb in Dutch oven or iron pot. Pour
in enough boiling water to cover meat by 1″.
Cover and cook on stove at medium heat for 2
hours or until tender. After the first hour of
cooking, add prepared vegetables. Season
with salt and pepper. One half hour before
serving, add potatoes. Cover and continue to
cook until all vegetables and meat are tender.
Turn off heat. Strain any fat from surface. In a
separate bowl, mix flour and cold water until
smooth. Add to stew. Turn heat up to medium
high and cook, stirring constantly until gravy
thickens (about 5 minutes). Adjust seasoning
and serve.

✳

*S*ix children and a husband presented a challenge: I had to cover three meals a day, twelve months a year. Certain criteria had to be met: a) my husband had to like it; just one little grimace from him caused a ripple effect called "rejection." b) The kids had to like it. c) Since five of the kids were boys, meals had to fill them up, at least for the period of time it took for them to wash the dishes and parade back and forth to the fridge to see what else was edible.

One of the most appreciated meals was Irish stew, my grandmother's version, which filled the kitchen with delicious aromas and promises of warmth inside and outside. Winters in New York on the East River were bitter; after sleigh riding, a bowl of stew and homemade bread took the kids' minds off of their frozen toes. The preparation of the stew was a ritual that required exact ingredients. Selecting the proper cut of lamb ensured the stew would not be fatty. A Dutch oven (iron pot) was a must. My grandmother's Irish stew was always a hit, providing many special evenings for my children, and now, for my grandchildren.

Alice McKechnie

WAS BORN ON OCTOBER 19, 1922,
IN ASTORIA, NEW YORK. SHE HAS SIX
CHILDREN AND SEVEN GRANDCHILDREN.

✳ *Beef Pasties* ✳

WINNIE THAISEN

FOR THE NEVER-FAIL PIECRUST:

3 cups all-purpose flour (never, *ever* use
   bread flour)

1 teaspoon salt

1 cup lard (best, though Crisco will do)

1 egg

1 tablespoon lemon juice

6 tablespoons water

FOR THE FILLING:

4 or 5 medium potatoes

5 or 6 big carrots

2 or 3 medium onions

½ small rutabaga

1 pound sirloin steak, diced

Season-All

Salt and pepper

3 teaspoons butter

To make the piecrust: Mix the flour, salt, and lard with a pastry blender (two table knives work okay, too). Mix until, when you pick up a handful, it will stick together.

With a fork or whisk, beat the egg, then stir in the lemon juice (you may substitute vinegar) and water. Stir this into the flour mixture with a fork until all of the mixture is picked up.

Divide the dough into 4 or 5 balls, according to the size of your pie plates. Chill dough 2 to 3 hours or overnight. Roll out one ball of dough to fit 9-inch or 10-inch glass pie pan and place in pan, allowing a 1-inch overhang on all sides. Spoon the filling inside. Roll another ball of dough to fit on top of pasty as the top crust. Before placing on filling, dot the mixture with butter.

To make the pasty: Dice the vegetables and put with the diced steak. (In a pinch you can use little hunks of lean ground beef or even diced tenderized steak.) Season well with Season-All and salt and pepper.

Preheat conventional oven to 375°F. Poke top crust with a fork in three or four spots. (The steam that forms helps cook the contents, so you don't want too much to escape.) Place on filling and press edges of top and bottom crusts together to seal.

Start in a microwave oven for 12 minutes on high, turning halfway through. Finish off for up to 45 minutes in a conventional oven. (To check to see if the pasty is done, poke through the crust and taste a carrot.) Cut into wedges and serve.

Note: A great leftover and freezes well.

When I was a bride, I was bewailing to my uncle-by-marriage's sister Annie that my piecrust was like cardboard. She gave me this Never-Fail Piecrust recipe that I use for lots of dishes. I make pasties in pie plates rather than as individual ones to help cut down on the calories—that nasty word! Besides, it's easier.

Use plenty of flour when rolling out as thin as possible. (Just brush off excess flour.) Don't worry if you have to patch it, roll it over again. It gets great, anyhow. That is why it is called Never-Fail. I use this for fruit pies and for pasties.

Winnie Thaisen

WAS BORN ON FEBRUARY 21, 1923, IN HIBBING, MINNESOTA. SHE HAS TWO CHILDREN, SIX GRANDCHILDREN, AND ONE GREAT-GRANDCHILD.

✳ *Liz's Meatloaf* ✳

LIZ CARPENTER

FOR THE MEATLOAF:

2 pounds very lean ground meat
2 eggs, slightly beaten
1 teaspoon baking powder
1 cup milk
1 cup soft bread crumbs
½ pound raw bacon
1 tablespoon prepared horseradish
3 tablespoons minced onion
2 cloves garlic, minced fine
1 tablespoon salt
½ teaspoon pepper
Fresh parsley, minced

FOR THE SAUCE:

1 tablespoon Worcestershire sauce
½ cup ketchup
1 teaspoon lemon juice

Preheat oven to 350°F. Mix the beef with the eggs, baking powder, milk, and bread crumbs. Chop the bacon (reserving 2 strips) and add, along with the remaining ingredients for the meatloaf. Shape in an 11 × 8-inch baking pan.

Mix the ingredients for the sauce and spread sauce over the meatloaf. Place the remaining strips of bacon on top and bake for about 1 hour.

✳

*G*rowing up in the Depression, meatloaf
was Sunday fare, while pork and beans
and rice were served daily with biscuits.
My mother washed her hands carefully and then
mixed up all the meatloaf ingredients thoroughly.
The secret ingredient which might improve the dish
is 1 teaspoon of baking powder, which, with the
eggs, makes the meatloaf looser and more porous.
We loved meatloaf time. This is a healthful and
filling dish, particularly if served with mashed
potatoes or rice.

Liz Carpenter

**WAS BORN ON SEPTEMBER 1, 1920, IN
SALADO, TEXAS. SHE HAS TWO CHILDREN
AND TWO GRANDCHILDREN.**

✻ *Spicy Brisket of Beef* ✻

NANCY CONRAD

8 pounds brisket
Salt and pepper
2 teaspoons garlic powder
4 large white onions
2 bay leaves
4–6 tomatoes, finely chopped
4 small red potatoes, optional
Mushrooms, optional

Preheat oven to 500°F. Season the meat with salt and pepper to taste and the garlic powder. Slice onions thin and place onions and bay leaves at the bottom of a roasting pan or covered roaster. Place brisket on top of onions and sear both sides of meat.

Reduce oven temperature to 325°F. Pour the tomatoes over top of the brisket. Cover the pan and slow-cook, making sure liquid is adequate. Add water as necessary. Cook for 3 hours. You may add pared and quartered potatoes or sliced mushrooms for the last hour of roasting.

Yield: 6 servings

Note: This dish is best if prepared the day before. After meat has cooled, refrigerate it. Before reheating, skim the fat. Slice the meat thin and return to the sauce. Reheat in 350°F. oven for 30 minutes.

Note: The modified ingredients consist of substituting 2 cans (8 ounces each) of tomato sauce and 2 packets of Lipton onion soup mix for the fresh tomatoes and the bay leaves. When using modified ingredients, there is no need to season the meat before cooking.

✻

One of my fondest childhood memories was going to my grandmother's house for dinner. Her special dish was Spicy Brisket of Beef. To make her special sauce she used fresh tomatoes, a combination of herbs, mushrooms, and brown gravy. By the time I got the recipe from my mother, the ingredients had been modified, and made easier, with canned tomato sauce and packaged onion soup mix. The fun began when my son moved to Prague, in the Czech Republic. Yearning for the taste of home, he phoned to ask me for my brisket recipe. Thanks to today's technology, I of course sent it to him by e-mail. (My grandmother would have had a good laugh.) However, grocery shopping in Prague posed some problems. My son had to modify my recipe with fresh tomatoes, a combination of herbs, mushrooms, and brown gravy. Which only goes to prove — what goes around, comes around.

Nancy Conrad

WAS BORN ON SEPTEMBER 25, 1942, IN DENVER, COLORADO. SHE HAS SIX CHILDREN (FOUR OF THEM STEPCHILDREN) AND SEVEN STEP-GRANDCHILDREN.

✳ *Deviled Short Ribs* ✳

ESTHER WILLIAMS SNYDER

1–2 tablespoons vegetable oil
3 pounds beef short ribs (boneless)
2 medium onions, chopped
½ cup Heinz chili sauce
½ cup beef broth
3 tablespoons cider vinegar
1½ tablespoons brown sugar
2 teaspoons Worcestershire sauce
1 teaspoon Dijon mustard
1 teaspoon dry mustard
1 teaspoon chili powder
1 teaspoon paprika
1 clove garlic, minced
½ teaspoon salt
½ teaspoon pepper
½–¾ cup of Burgundy
2 bay leaves

Preheat oven to 275°F. Heat oil in large Dutch oven on stove top and brown ribs in it a few at a time. Remove them to a large platter as they are cooked. Discard accumulated fat. Return all ribs to Dutch oven and remove from heat. In a large bowl combine all remaining ingredients. Pour over ribs. Cover and bake for 3 hours at 275°F until tender when pierced with a fork.

When I was growing up in Kansas City, our wonderful cook Alpha used to make this dish. When I got married, all I knew how to make was fudge. Years later, I started making this dish. I cooked it for my family. I haven't made it for a long time now, because my grandchildren eat only chicken, fish, and vegetables. This dish is what I make for older people, like myself, who still love red meat.

Esther Williams Snyder

WAS BORN ESTHER GRANT WILLIAMS IN
KANSAS CITY, MISSOURI, ON MARCH 8, 1915.
SHE HAS TWO CHILDREN AND FOUR
GRANDCHILDREN.

✳ *Pork Chops and Applesauce* ✳

CORINNE WILEY

1 tablespoon oil
4 center-cut pork chops
1 cup diced celery
1 green pepper, cut into small pieces
1 yellow onion, sliced
1 cup rice
2 ¼ cups consommé
Salt and pepper
Tabasco
Applesauce

Heat oil in a skillet until hot, but not smoking, and sear the pork chops on both sides. Reduce heat to medium and add the celery. Put green pepper, onion, rice, and consommé, together with the chops, into an electric skillet, or put into a casserole and place in a preheated 350°F. oven. Cook approximately 1 hour or until consommé is absorbed. Season to taste with salt, pepper, and a few drops of Tabasco.

Serve with applesauce.

M any Hollywood stars — Clark Gable, John Wayne, Randolph Scott — used to stay at a fabulous Minden, Nevada, ranch that belonged to cousins of mine. At the age of twelve, I had the opportunity to move cattle from Minden up to Hope Valley for summer grazing. I rode tail, or back of the herd, arriving for chow late — black with dust, tongue sticking to the roof of my mouth, and so stiff I could hardly walk after fourteen hours in the saddle. Our dinner that night was this dish. It has been a favorite ever since and always brings back great memories.

Corinne Wiley

WAS BORN ON APRIL 30, 1931, IN
SAN FRANCISCO, CALIFORNIA. SHE HAS TWO
CHILDREN AND FIVE GRANDCHILDREN.

✴ *Nana's Divine Tamale Pie* ✴

MARYNELL PHILLIPS STONE

FOR THE BOTTOM LAYER:
½ cup yellow cornmeal
½ teaspoon salt
1 cup boiling water
1½ cups milk

FOR THE FILLING:
1 yellow onion, chopped
Bacon grease
2 tablespoons Grandma's Chili Powder*
2 heaping cups cubed cooked ham
1 can cream-style corn
1 large can whole solid-pack tomatoes
1 can (3–6 ounces) pitted black olives, sliced

FOR THE TOPPING:
1 regular-size package corn muffin mix, or 2 small packages (Jiffy)

To make the bottom layer: Stir the cornmeal and salt into the boiling water in the top of a double boiler placed over open flame. Stir the mixture until it begins to thicken. Add the milk. Stir gently and set the pot into the lower pot of the double boiler, over hot water. Simmer, covered, for 30 minutes. Line the bottom of a well-greased 2-quart flat baking dish with this mixture. Cool.

To make the filling: Sauté the onion in the bacon grease. Sprinkle the chili powder over onion and add the cubed ham, corn, and tomatoes, including fairly large pieces of tomato. Blend thoroughly.

Spoon filling carefully on top of the cornmeal when that layer is firm and cool in the baking dish. Dot with the olives and refrigerate.

To make the topping and the Tamale Pie: Preheat oven to 375°F. Just before baking, make corn muffin mix according to directions on the package. Spread on top of the filling.

Bake the Tamale Pie at 375°F for 15 minutes, or until the top is lightly browned. Then turn the oven down to 325°F for 40 minutes longer so the pie can cook slowly. Cover pie loosely with foil if top gets too brown. Should look golden on top.

***Yield:* 6 ample servings**

*Grandma's Chili Powder is a product of Grandma's Spanish Pepper Company. It's available in supermarkets and grocery stores.

Note: This casserole can be made a day in advance, except for the topping of corn muffin mix. As a leftover, it is delicious hot or cold.

✴

This is a very festive recipe passed down through my mother's mother, Nana Pauline Gallerine. She was of French and German descent, a very gracious, loving person that everyone adored and loved to visit as a guest in her home. She was generous to a fault. This recipe was her aunt's, passed down and embellished, and loved by all who indulged. As youngsters we begged for it, as teenagers we still requested it, and all of our dating gentlemen, our uncles, and men in general always asked for it. They especially loved it cold the next day.

Marynell Phillips Stone

WAS BORN ON AUGUST 12, 1937, IN PORTLAND, OREGON. SHE HAS TWO CHILDREN AND THREE GRANDCHILDREN.

✳ *Pizza Ripieno* (Stuffed Pizza) ✳

CONCETTA TROPIANO

FOR THE PIZZA DOUGH:

1 package active dry yeast, or ½–¾ cake
    fresh yeast
½ cup warm water plus 1½ cups
4 cups all-purpose flour
1 tablespoon salt

FOR THE PIZZA RIPIENO:

4 cups chopped picnic ham (pork
    shoulder butt)
1 container (15 ounces) whole milk ricotta
    cheese
¼ cup grated pecorino Romano
1 large (12 ounces) whole milk mozzarella,
    shredded
Salt and pepper
Flour (for the board)
Cornmeal (for the pan)

To make the dough: Dissolve the yeast in ½ cup warm water. In a large bowl, combine the flour and salt, make a well in the center, and add yeast mixture. Mix with a fork while adding enough of the remaining water to combine dough. Mix, using hands and adding more water or flour as necessary. The dough should not be too sticky. Knead slightly. Place in a clean, large bowl and cover with plastic wrap and a towel. Place bowl in a warm place and allow to rise for about 2 hours. The dough should double in size.

To make the Pizza Ripieno: Preheat oven to 350°F. Combine the ingredients for the filling. Check for seasonings.

Sprinkle a 13 × 9-inch pan with cornmeal. Divide the pizza dough in half. Flour the board and roll out one half of dough to desired thickness. Place in the pan. Spread with the filling. Roll out the remaining dough. Place on top of filling in pan. Seal the edges, using a fork to press both doughs together. Bake for 1 hour, until dough is slightly brown and thoroughly baked. This ham pie is usually made during the Easter holiday.

Note: Before it is chopped, the ham butt can be boiled for 1 hour in a large pot of water to remove some of the salt. Salami or prosciutto can replace the ham.

✳

I n addition to raising five children and working in a factory, I helped my husband take care of a mini farm, raising cows, goats, and chickens and bottling my own tomatoes and jellies. We used to have an outdoor oven in which I made bread and biscotti. I still make these, but in a conventional oven now. Recently, I've had a stroke and a heart attack, but I still make pizza, homemade pasta, and biscotti once a week. I love to cook for friends and family. My grandchildren are always asking for my recipes.

Concetta Tropiano

WAS BORN ON DECEMBER 8, 1908, IN CITTANUOVA, ITALY. SHE HAS FIVE CHILDREN, FOURTEEN GRANDCHILDREN, SIXTEEN GREAT-GRANDCHILDREN, AND THREE STEP-GREAT-GRANDCHILDREN.

Vegetable Corn Casserole

NANCY S. SCHNELLER

2 eggs, slightly beaten

1¼ cups milk

2½ cups corn kernels, fresh or frozen

2 chopped peeled tomatoes

1 green pepper, chopped

4 ounces pimiento

½ cup sliced pitted black olives

1 cup yellow cornmeal

1 teaspoon salt

¼ teaspoon pepper

¼ teaspoon paprika

¼ teaspoon chili powder

1 small onion, chopped, optional

4 ounces (1 stick) butter or margarine, melted

Preheat oven to 350°F. Combine the eggs, milk, corn, tomato, green pepper, pimiento, olives, cornmeal, salt, pepper, paprika, chili powder, and onion. Pour the melted butter into the mixture. Mix well and pour into an oiled 2-quart casserole dish.

Bake uncovered for 60 minutes.

This is a classic grandmother recipe when all the required veggies are in season. A really ambitious cook can use fresh corn instead of frozen. My sister gave me this recipe, and the two of us have given it to our daughters — six of them, combined. It's healthy and make-aheadable.

Nancy S. Schneller

WAS BORN ON APRIL 7, 1924, IN HARTFORD, CONNECTICUT. SHE HAS THREE CHILDREN AND SIX GRANDCHILDREN.

Tourlou-Tourlou (Greek Braised Vegetables)

ALEXANDRA PANOUSIS

5 fresh artichokes
Juice of 2 lemons
4–5 tomatoes
2 onions, sliced
4 cloves garlic, crushed
½ cup olive oil
1 pound string beans, trimmed
1 cup water plus additional for
    soaking artichokes
6 peeled carrots, cut lengthwise, then in half
1 green bell pepper, diced
2 Japanese eggplants, sliced
2 zucchini, sliced
2 peeled potatoes, cut in ½-inch diamonds
1 package frozen lima beans
4 tablespoons Italian parsley, snipped
Salt and pepper

Peel the artichokes to their hearts; discard the leaves. Cover the artichoke hearts with water and the lemon juice. Soak overnight.

Submerge tomatoes in boiling water for a few seconds, then remove from water and peel and chop. Preheat oven to 400°F. In a large pot, sauté the onion and garlic in the olive oil. Add the tomatoes and cook until soft. Add the string beans and cook for approximately 5 minutes, stirring frequently. Add the 1 cup of water.

Put the string bean mixture and carrots on the bottom of a large baking dish. Drain artichokes and add to dish. Add the remaining vegetables, and add salt and pepper to taste. Put pan on the stovetop over two burners to simmer for approximately 15 minutes. Don't stir.

Bake uncovered for 1 hour, or until vegetables are tender and there is no remaining liquid in pan.

I really enjoy making this dish, because the vegetables always turn out to be so tasty. I like this particular recipe because it is different than the usual ways of preparing vegetables—steamed, boiled, or stewed, how boring! These baked vegetables are easy to prepare and always are delicious.

I first learned how to prepare this recipe by watching my mother make it for our family. We had an oven outside. She baked the vegetables in this oven. This was in the old country, Greece, in our village, Vassiliko. I think of my mother whenever I make Tourlou-Tourlou.

I'm glad to be in America. I have always been grateful for the modern conveniences. I love to cook. It's my hobby. I don't cook because I like to eat, I cook because I like to make other people happy.

Alexandra Panousis

WAS BORN ON APRIL 15, 1912, IN VASSILIKO, GREECE. SHE IMMIGRATED TO THE UNITED STATES WHEN SHE WAS TWENTY-TWO. SHE HAD THREE CHILDREN (ONE IS NOW DECEASED) AND THREE GRANDCHILDREN.

✳ *Mrs. White's Spinach Patties* ✳

CARMELLA R. EVERETT

4 packages fresh spinach, approximately
  2 pounds fresh
4 eggs
2½ cups white or whole wheat flour
1 medium onion, chopped
½ teaspoon salt
½ teaspoon pepper
Garlic salt, optional
Oil for frying

Boil the spinach until tender, then drain and chop coarsely. Add the eggs, flour, onion, salt and pepper, and garlic salt. Mix well.

Use 2 tablespoons (or desired portion) of mixture for each pattie. Fry in hot oil, turning once, until brown on both sides. This can be used as a side dish or a main dish.

Yield: about 18 patties

I grew up living in my grandparents' house with my parents, brother, and grandparents. My grandparents, who came from Italy, built their own brick home, and had a large garden and grapevines, cherry trees, pear trees, and apricot trees. We had fresh chicken, fresh eggs, and milk from our own goat. My grandmother loved to cook. She made her own pasta, cakes, bread, wine, jelly, soap, and root beer soda. This recipe — my favorite — is the only way my grandmother got her family to eat spinach, and I have followed in her footsteps with my family.

Carmella R. Everett

WAS BORN ON MAY 4, 1938, IN NEW BRUNSWICK, NEW JERSEY. SHE HAS TWO CHILDREN AND TWO GRANDCHILDREN.

✳ *Green Tomato Pie* ✳

DOROTHY O'NEAL

5 large green tomatoes
1 tablespoon butter
1 cup sugar
2 tablespoons vinegar
1 teaspoon nutmeg
1 tablespoon flour
$\frac{1}{4}$ cup water plus additional for
   cooking the tomatoes
Pastry for a 2-crust pie

Preheat oven to 375°F. Peel and thinly slice the tomatoes. Cook slowly with the butter until tender. (A small amount of water may need to be added.) When done, stir in the sugar, vinegar, and nutmeg.

Make a paste of the flour and the $\frac{1}{4}$ cup water and add to the tomato mixture. Turn into an unbaked pie crust and top with the upper crust. Bake as any fruit pie, for 30 minutes or until nicely browned.

My grandmother, who lived to be 104, and my mother were two of my biggest inspirations in learning how to cook, keep house, and find out what family is all about. My grandmother Brown made Green Tomato Pie that was out of this world. She had two secrets: The first was choosing large green tomatoes that had turned white on the bottom (this prevented bitterness). The second was cooking the tomatoes before baking the pie.

Dorothy O'Neal

WAS BORN ON DECEMBER 19, 1932, IN VALIER, MONTANA. SHE HAS THREE CHILDREN AND SIX GRANDCHILDREN.

✳ *Mushroom Pie* ✳

LEILA H. SCOTT

3 tablespoons butter or margarine
1 cup sliced onions
1½ pounds mushrooms, washed and sliced
   (any combination of button mushrooms,
   shiitake, oyster, portobello, or crimini)
½ teaspoon Worcestershire sauce
1 tablespoon lemon juice
1 teaspoon salt
Pepper
½ pound Swiss cheese, shredded
1 package piecrust for a 2-crust pie, or a
   crust of your own (Use Never-Fail
   Piecrust. See Beef Pasties, page 56)
1 egg yolk
1 tablespoon water

Preheat oven to 375°F. Melt the butter in a skillet. Add the onions, mushrooms, Worcestershire sauce, lemon juice, salt, and a dash of pepper. Cook for 5 minutes. Drain very well.

Combine the mushroom mixture and the cheese really well and turn into an unbaked pie shell. Arrange the pastry strips in lattice fashion on top of the filling. Beat the egg yolk and water together and brush over the pastry.

Bake for 35 to 40 minutes, or until golden brown.

✳

When I was a girl in Red Bank, New Jersey, all grandmothers cooked from scratch. My mother cooked the same dinners her mother would make. Mother would also cook the things that my father's mother used to make when he was a boy. Dad would tell Mother what to use, in what quantity, to get the taste that he remembered. There were no cookbooks to use back in those days. My father's mother came from Hungary, and through the years there were some dinners and pastry desserts that I wish I had written down. This recipe for Mushroom Pie was used by my mother at her church men's club dinners.

Leila H. Scott

WAS BORN ON SEPTEMBER 28, 1941, IN RED BANK, NEW JERSEY. SHE HAS SIX CHILDREN AND NINE GRANDCHILDREN.

✳ *Grandpa Harry Rubin's Pickles* ✳

RUTH RUBIN ADELMAN

PICKLED CUCUMBERS:

50 pounds pickling cucumbers

2 pounds kosher salt

Water to cover cucumbers in a container
(preferably a barrel)

½ pound pickling spices

1 pound crushed garlic cloves

6 bunches fresh dill, left whole

Put the cucumbers in a barrel. Dissolve the salt with water. Pour over the cucumbers. Add the pickling spices, garlic, and dill. Cover, with lid held directly atop the cucumbers with a rock, to keep the pickles in the brine. Cure for at least 1 to 2 weeks — the longer you cure, the more sour they become.

PICKLED TOMATOES:

50 pounds green tomatoes

3½ pounds kosher salt

Water to cover the tomatoes in a
container (preferably a barrel)

¾ pound pickling spices

2 bunches celery

2 pounds garlic, crushed

1½ quarts white vinegar

Put the tomatoes in a barrel. Dissolve the salt with water. Pour over the tomatoes. Add the other ingredients on top. There should be enough brine to overflow onto the cover of the barrel. Cover *lightly*. It should take 2 weeks to pickle. Keep pickles at a cool temperature after they are cured.

When I was growing up, my parents had a store on Essex Street in Lower Manhattan. There, the recipes were perfected. My fondest memory is of my father leaving at 3 A.M. for an all-day outing to Long Island to visit farms and pick up the vegetables needed for pickling. I laugh now remembering my teachers from Seward High School threatening to fail me if they didn't get good pickles after school. I passed all my courses.

Ruth Rubin Adelman

WAS BORN ON JUNE 5, 1920, IN
NEW YORK CITY. SHE HAS TWO CHILDREN
AND THREE GRANDCHILDREN.

Green Tomato Relish

GLORIA R. NATALE

12 green tomatoes (medium to large)
5 green peppers
3 large onions
3 cups cider vinegar
1 cup flour
5 cups white sugar
2 tablespoons salt
2 tablespoons turmeric
2 tablespoons celery seed
1 small jar prepared mustard (French's)

Wash the tomatoes, core, and cut into quarters. Wash the green peppers, core, remove seeds, and cut into segments. Peel the onions, then cut into quarters. Grind, using a coarse grinding plate. Catch in a colander and drain.

Put the drained vegetables into a large, heavy sauce pot. Add the vinegar and bring to a boil. Meanwhile, in a medium bowl, mix the flour with the sugar. Add the salt, turmeric, and celery seed and have this mixture ready.

Stir the mustard into the flour mixture to make a paste. Add to the boiling vegetables. Bring to a boil again and time for 10 minutes.

Have sterilized, 6 quart-size canning jars ready. Keep them hot in simmering water. Keep the lids hot in simmering water also.

Have ready a towel, rack, tongs, wide-mouth funnel, and a clean cloth for wiping jars before sealing.

Ladle the hot mixture into the hot jars. Fill each jar to about 1 inch from the top. Wipe down the jar. Put on a hot lid and place ring on and tighten. Lids should go up, then down, to create a vacuum seal.

Yield: **6 quarts**

Gloria R. Natale

WAS BORN ON AUGUST 1, 1931, IN
PITTSBURGH, PENNSYLVANIA. SHE HAS
FOUR CHILDREN AND SEVEN
GRANDCHILDREN.

Both my maternal and paternal grandparents owned hotels and served three meals a day in the dining rooms. I grew up loving to cook. I taught home economics for twenty-six years after my children were all in school. When I visit my grandchildren or they visit me, we cook. This recipe is one that my grandma McDonald passed on to my mother and now to me. It is an excellent use for those green tomatoes left at the end of summer. When my students made this, they said it reminded them of visiting their grandmothers who canned. They loved the "smells."

* *Pepper Relish* *

MARION PAYNE

6 green peppers
6 red peppers
3 onions, peeled and coarsely chopped
1 cup sugar
2 teaspoons salt
1 tablespoon celery seed
1½ cups vinegar

Remove the seeds and white pith from the peppers. Put the peppers and the chopped onions through a food chopper, using medium blade.

Cover with boiling water, let stand 5 minutes, then drain well. Add sugar, salt, celery seed, and vinegar. Bring to boil. Boil gently for 20 minutes.

Pour into hot sterilized jars. Seal according to the manufacturer's exact instructions.

Yield: **8 cups**

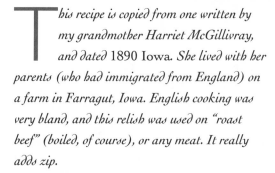

This recipe is copied from one written by my grandmother Harriet McGillivray, and dated 1890 Iowa. She lived with her parents (who had immigrated from England) on a farm in Farragut, Iowa. English cooking was very bland, and this relish was used on "roast beef" (boiled, of course), or any meat. It really adds zip.

Every fall, after harvesting the green peppers and onions, Grandma made 60 to 80 pints of this relish. Many jars were given as gifts at Christmas.

Marion Payne

WAS BORN ON AUGUST 3, 1925, IN LONGMONT, COLORADO. SHE HAD TWO CHILDREN (ONE IS NOW DECEASED), AND HAS TWO GRANDCHILDREN.

✴

✳ *Mango Chutney* ✳

JOAN TRAVIS

½ pound onions
2 cloves garlic, peeled
½ pound green ginger, peeled
2 ounces yellow chili peppers
   (3 peppers plus a few seeds from
   each—the more seeds the hotter)
1 quart Japanese rice vinegar
3 pounds brown sugar
1 tablespoon salt
2 pounds currants
2 pounds raisins
4 pounds (7 medium-size) mangoes
   (firm but neither too green nor quite
   ready to eat)
1 cup shelled pine nuts

Making chutney differs from making jams and jellies in several important ways.

1. The only limit to the size of the batch is the size of the pot.

2. It is a two-phase operation: Ingredients are prepared and combined and allowed to stand, covered, overnight.

3. You need *not* stir constantly (as with jams and jellies). But *do* stir occasionally to keep all parts of the batch circulating, and to avoid sticking.

DAY 1: Combine the onions, garlic, ginger, and chili peppers with some of the vinegar and process in a blender or food processor until the mixture becomes slushy. Put into a large pot.

Add the brown sugar, salt, currants, raisins, the remaining vinegar, and the mangoes, and *stir* until thoroughly mixed. Cover the pot with a cloth and let stand overnight.

DAY 2: Add the pine nuts to the pot. Stir thoroughly and bring to a rapid boil. Boil the mixture until it is thick and gloppy (about 45 minutes), stirring occasionally to be sure it is well mixed and isn't sticking to the bottom of the pot. Meanwhile, sterilize 12 pint-size jars and keep them hot.

To test the thickening process, put a few spoonfuls of the mixture in a saucer. Allow it to cool slightly, then run a finger through it. If it keeps an open pathway, it is ready to put into the hot sterilized jars. Fill the jars. Be sure the rims are clean—free of chutney or juice—to assure a complete seal. Tighten the lids as much as possible. Tidy up the outside of the jars in case some of the syrupy juice has gotten on the sides. Let stand until cool and lids have made a popping sound, as this will signify a perfect seal. Once a jar has been opened, you should refrigerate the unused portion.

In California, where I have lived for many years, Mexican and Hawaiian mangoes are available and reasonably priced during most of June and July. So, to segue from fresh to preserved is easy.

This recipe may be practically foolproof, but beware of inviting too many appreciative friends to help you make a batch with and for them. This is *not* a quilting bee. A team might reduce peeling and chopping time, but problems arise which also reduce the likelihood of producing a superior product. (I tried it with four friends — never again!) My chutney, with its mango base, is treasured by friends and family, and is heavenly with just about anything — from curries to roast beef to cottage cheese.

Joan Travis

WAS BORN ON JUNE 4, 1924, IN MINNEAPOLIS, MINNESOTA. SHE HAS BEEN MARRIED FIFTY-THREE AND THREE-QUARTER YEARS TO THE SAME MAN AND HAS ONE CHILD AND TWO GRANDCHILDREN.

✻ *Obachan's Special Teriyaki Sauce*✻

OKOTO GOTAN

1 slice gingerroot, ½ inch thick
1 slice peeled yellow onion, 1 inch thick
   (about 3 tablespoons when grated)
3 or 4 peeled garlic cloves
1 cup soy sauce (low-sodium soy sauce may
   be substituted)
1 cup sugar
½ cup mirin (Japanese rice wine)

Using narrowest opening of a grater, grate gingerroot, onion, and garlic. Combine all ingredients.

Use sauce to marinate chicken, meat, vegetables for at least 1 hour before broiling or char-grilling.

I n 1924, my husband and I were married in Hiroshima, Japan. We immigrated to the Sacramento Valley, where we farmed for many years. During World War II, we were interned in Jerome and also Rohr, Arkansas. After that we relocated temporarily to Chicago. Ultimately we returned to our farm in Florin, where I still live.

Obachan means "honorable grandmother" in Japanese. This recipe has been used in the family for decades. It is a "special" recipe because only on special occasions, such as holidays, are the onion, ginger, and garlic added to the sauce. My grandchildren ask me, Why, when the recipe is already so simple? I tell them, if you add the special ingredients all the time, it wouldn't be special.

Okoto Gotan
(seated)

WAS BORN ON JANUARY 6, 1907, IN HIROSHIMA, JAPAN. SHE HAS FOUR CHILDREN, FIVE GRANDCHILDREN, AND THREE GREAT-GRANDCHILDREN.

✳ *Grape Jelly* ✳

BERNETA W. BIVENS

4 pounds Concord grapes, stemmed
1½ cups water
1 box Sure-Jell
7 cups sugar
1 box paraffin (found next to the Sure-Jell)

Place grapes in a deep 8-quart steel pan. Cover with water and cook over medium heat until the skins burst, about 10 minutes. Line a large, cone-shaped strainer with cheesecloth and place over another large saucepan. Pour grapes with all liquid into strainer, allowing juice to drain. When almost all the juice is extracted, push gently on the grapes to extract a total of 5 cups of juice.

Bring the juice to a full boil and stir in Sure-Jell. Boil 1 minute. Add all sugar and, stirring constantly with a wooden spoon, bring mixture back up to a boil and boil another minute *only*.

Remove from heat and skim off foam with a metal spoon. Pour into four sterilized pint-size jars and let cool for 12 hours, covered loosely with a towel. When cool, pour a ¼-inch layer of melted paraffin on top and cover with lids.

Yield: 4 pints jelly

✳

Berneta Bivens

WAS BORN ON MARCH 17, 1898, IN
HARRISONVILLE, MISSOURI. SHE HAS TWO
CHILDREN, TWO GRANDCHILDREN, AND
TWO GREAT-GRANDCHILDREN.

I prepare this jelly and other preserves in my kitchen at Coldwater Ranch, my favorite spot where I spend my summers with my daughter and grandson. I also have a large garden to share with my friends.

✳ *Grandma Bessie's Apple Pie* ✳

BESSIE CECIL

FOR THE CRUST:

3 cups all-purpose flour
1 level teaspoon salt
1 cup Crisco shortening
2 egg yolks, beaten (for glaze)
4 tablespoons ice water

FOR THE FILLING:

6–8 firm Gravenstein or Granny Smith
   apples
2 tablespoons lemon juice
½ cup packed brown sugar, or
   ⅓ cup granulated
3 tablespoons all-purpose flour
½ teaspoon cinnamon
Nutmeg
2 tablespoons cold unsalted butter,
   cut into small pieces

To make the dough: Sift and measure the flour. Mix the salt into the flour with a pastry blender. Add the Crisco and continue blending until the dough is crumbly. I prefer my dough a little bit on the damp side. Mix 2 yolks with ice water and add to mixture, tossing lightly with a fork just until dough comes together.

This will make enough for 1 double-crust pie and 1 extra crust—not a double pie, though. (For each crust measure 1 cup of mixture.) Cool dough in the refrigerator.

To make the filling: Peel, core, and slice the apples. Squeeze the lemon juice over the apples and toss together. In separate bowl, blend the sugar with the flour. Next, add the cinnamon and a little nutmeg. Mix and add to the apples.

To assemble the pie: Preheat oven to 425°F. Cut off one third of dough and place between two pieces of wax paper. Roll from the middle towards all sides. You have to pull off the paper each time it clings to the dough. Use flour if it sticks. Gently lift and place in a 9-inch pie dish. Poke several holes in the bottom of the crust. Fill the bottom crust with the apple filling. Even out the mixture by mounding towards the middle. Dot the top of the fruit with 6 to 8 small chunks of butter. Cut off a second portion of the dough and roll out the top crust. Cover the filling, pinching the top crust together with the bottom crust. Poke several small holes into the piecrust.

Place the pie into the oven at 425°. After 15 minutes, lower the temperature to 375°F. and cook for about 30 minutes, or until brown.

This is the pie that inspired the book.

t all seems so simple, but can be a real mess if one doesn't do it this way. Don't give up on the wax paper sticking to the dough. Just pull apart three or four times on both sides each time. Soon you will see it's simple when you get on to it—and it does take patience for us neurotics— but this is it. Read this two or three times before you start and it will go well. Don't handle the dough too much.

Bessie Cecil
WAS BORN ON
FEBRUARY 13, 1902,
ON GREENLEAF RANCH IN
KINGMAN, KANSAS. SHE HAS
FIVE CHILDREN, THIRTEEN
GRANDCHILDREN AND THIRTEEN
GREAT-GRANDCHILDREN.

✳ *Cherry Pie* ✳

FOR THE FILLING:

1 bag (20 ounces) frozen pitted
   red cherries, juice reserved
1½ cups sugar, divided
⅓ cup cornstarch
⅛ teaspoon salt
½ cup raspberry juice cocktail
1 tablespoon butter
½ teaspoon red food coloring
¼ teaspoon almond extract

FOR THE CRUST:

2 cups flour
¾ teaspoon salt
¾ cup Crisco shortening
¼ cup ice water
1 teaspoon white vinegar
Sugar (for top)

To make the filling: Thaw and thoroughly drain the cherries, reserving ½ cup of the juice. Combine ¾ cup of the sugar with the cornstarch and salt in a medium saucepan. Add the reserved cherry juice and raspberry juice cocktail. Cook and stir over medium heat until mixture thickens and is smooth and clear. Remove from heat. Add the remaining ¾ cup sugar, along with the butter, food col-

oring, almond extract, and cherries. Stir until the sugar is dissolved. Set aside to cool while preparing the crust.

To make the dough: Combine the flour and salt in a medium bowl. Cut in shortening with a pastry blender to form pea-sized chunks. Combine the water and vinegar and stir in with a fork until the dough forms a ball.

To assemble the pie: Preheat oven to 425°F. Using half the dough, roll out to fit a 9-inch pie plate. Trim edge. Fill the pie shell with the cooled filling. Roll the rest of the dough to fit top of pie with a ¾-inch overhang. Turn crust under to seal. Flute edges of crust and make several slits in top crust to release steam. Sprinkle the crust with sugar. Wrap crust edge with 2-inch strips of foil to prevent overbrowning.

Bake at 425°F. for 15 minutes. Reduce temperature to 400°F. and continue baking for about 40 minutes. Remove from oven. Cool. Remove foil strips. Cool to room temperature.

✳

*A*s I approached the age of becoming a "Senior," and needing some new activities in my life, I began to enter cooking contests, especially those that called for original recipes. This cherry pie was a big winner for me and really got me going on a fun and rewarding hobby. My personalized license plate reads: *PIE BAKER.*

Eunice Ruth

WAS BORN ON DECEMBER 19, 1933, IN SURPRISE, NEBRASKA. SHE HAS THREE CHILDREN AND TWO GRANDCHILDREN.

French Rhubarb Pie ✳

ELIZABETH STOLTZFUS

FOR THE PIE:

1 egg, beaten

¾–1 cup granulated brown sugar

1 teaspoon vanilla

2 cups rhubarb, trimmed and cut in
   1-inch slices

2 tablespoons flour

1 unbaked 9-inch pie shell (see page 92)

FOR THE CRUMB TOPPING:

1 cup flour

½ cup brown sugar

½ teaspoon baking soda

½ teaspoon baking powder

2 tablespoons butter

Preheat oven to 375°F. Crumble all topping ingredients together in a small bowl until the texture of cornmeal. Combine all filling ingredients and pour into unbaked pie shell. Sprinkle evenly with topping and bake for 40 to 45 minutes until filling is bubbly and topping is browned.

✳

used this recipe for a long time.
It was passed down to me by
my mother.

Elizabeth Stoltzfus

WAS BORN ON SEPTEMBER 4, 1923,
IN GORDONVILLE, PENNSYLVANIA. SHE
HAS EIGHT CHILDREN, THIRTY-
FIVE GRANDCHILDREN, AND SIX
GREAT-GRANDCHILDREN.

✳ *Grand Champion Lemon Pie* ✳

ROSE ANNE SACHSE

FOR THE CRUST:

10 tablespoons shortening
1½ cups flour
½ teaspoon salt
¼ teaspoon ground mace
3–4 tablespoons ice water

FOR THE FILLING:

3 egg yolks
1¼ cups sugar
3 tablespoons cornstarch
Salt
3 tablespoons fresh lemon juice
1½ cups hot water

FOR THE MERINGUE:

3 eggs whites
¼ teaspoon cream of tartar
5 tablespoons sugar
½ teaspoon vanilla

To make the crust: Preheat oven to 425°F. Cut the shortening into the dry ingredients with a pastry blender. Add the water sparingly, a little at a time. (Mother said, "Pretend that water costs a dollar a drop.")

Divide the dough in half and roll out one half for a 9-inch pie pan. Shape to pan, flute edges. Pierce sides and bottom with a fork.

Bake for about 10 minutes, or until golden brown. Cool to room temperature.

Note: I find that aluminum pie pans are still the best.

This piecrust recipe makes enough for a two-crust pie. I bake one and roll out the second one between two sheets of wax paper. Then I place on a pizza tin and freeze. I often keep six to eight unbaked crusts in the freezer in a large Ziploc bag.

To make the filling: Combine the egg yolks, sugar, cornstarch, salt, and lemon juice. Stir into the hot water and cook until thick and clear, stirring constantly. Cool slightly.

To make the meringue: With an electric mixer on high speed, beat the egg whites with the cream of tartar until peaks form. Gradually beat in the sugar, one tablespoon at a time. Add the vanilla and continue beating (with mixer on medium speed) until stiff peaks form.

To assemble the pie: Pour the filling into baked pie shell and cover with meringue, making sure you extend the meringue to the edge of the crust. Bake at 350°F. for 12 to 15 minutes, or until nicely browned.

Note: It is best to bake in advance and refrigerate pie so it will be nice and firm for serving.

My father, Frank X. Clarke from South Dakota, thought that lemon pie was the best pie in all the land. Mother made pies every week, but if there was special company or one of us girls brought home a young man that he approved of, he would stick his head in the kitchen door: "Mom, make a lemon pie for this young man." We still keep up the tradition and serve this Grand Champion Lemon Pie to favorite guests.

Rose Anne Sachse

WAS BORN ON MAY 1, 1929, IN ETHAN, SOUTH DAKOTA. SHE HAS FIVE CHILDREN AND FOUR GRANDCHILDREN.

Irene's Mincemeat

SHIRLEY CHEATUM

2 pounds lean beef, cooked
4 pounds apples
2½ pounds raisins
1½ pounds currants
¼ cup citron
½ pound ground suet
2 oranges
4 cups brown sugar
½ cup molasses
½ teaspoon ground cloves
1¼ teaspoons nutmeg
1½ teaspoons cinnamon
2 teaspoons salt
3 cups (about) meat broth or apple cider

Grind the beef, apples, raisins, currants, citron, suet, and oranges. Put into a large kettle. Mix together and add the brown sugar, molasses, and seasonings. Add broth until the mixture is moist.

Cook until the apples are tender. Put into hot sterilized jars and seal according to the manufacturer's exact instructions.

Yield: about 9 pints

This is my mother's mincemeat recipe. She always made a batch for pies at Thanksgiving. Occasionally she would add some apricot brandy. We all looked forward to dessert time and a piece of mincemeat pie. I guess the reason this is special is because I can remember my mom grinding up the ingredients and singing away while doing it. She was a happy person and an excellent cook. I've tried to keep the tradition going since her death.

Shirley Cheatum

WAS BORN ON SEPTEMBER 9, 1935, IN
LYONS, KANSAS. SHE HAS TWO CHILDREN
AND THREE GRANDCHILDREN.

Aunt Ruth's Devil's Food Cake

BETTY GARROD

½ cup butter (at room temperature)
2 cups sugar
3 eggs
2 cups cake flour
½ cup sour cream or buttermilk
½ cup cocoa
¾ cup cold coffee
1 teaspoon vanilla
1 teaspoon baking soda
2 tablespoons boiling water

Preheat oven to 350°F. Cream together the butter and sugar. Add the eggs, beating in one at a time. Alternately add flour and sour cream. Dissolve the cocoa in the coffee, then add to mixture, along with the vanilla. Lastly, dissolve the baking soda in the boiling water and add to mixture.

Spread the batter in a 13 × 9-inch pan. Bake for 35 to 40 minutes.

W hen I first married into the family, fifty-five years ago, whenever there was a family get-together, Aunt Ruth, my husband's aunt, had to bring her cake. It's now our family favorite. I have made it for a lot of special times, and most recently for a bakery prize.

Betty Garrod

WAS BORN ON MARCH 4, 1922, IN OMAHA, NEBRASKA. SHE HAS THREE CHILDREN, FIVE GRANDCHILDREN, AND FOUR GREAT-GRANDCHILDREN.

Crumb Cake

PAT MEIERHENRY

2 cups flour
1½ cups sugar
¾ cup butter
2 teaspoons baking powder
2 eggs
¾ cup milk

Preheat oven to 350°F. With hands, mix the flour, sugar, butter, and baking powder together into crumbs. Set one small cupful aside.

Break the eggs into the remainder of the crumbs. Add the milk and beat until the batter looks like cream. Pour into a long pan (13 × 9 inches). Sprinkle the reserved crumbs on the top.

Bake for about 30 minutes.

Note: Sometimes I've reduced the butter to ½ cup, the sugar to 1 cup, and used a 9-inch square pan.

I serve this in our bed-and-breakfast with strawberries, and everyone loves it. I am in the process of accumulating my favorite recipes for my kids. This cake, my own grandmother's crumb cake, is great because it's made from ingredients on hand and tastes best warm. It can be used as a coffee cake, a shortcake, or just a snack cake. My father, who otherwise could not cook, used to make this and eat it all himself.

I'm a hospice nurse. Lived on a farm for thirty years and raised kids and cows. I write a column, "The Farmer's Wife," for the local paper.

Pat Meierhenry

WAS BORN ON MAY 15, 1938, IN
YORK, NEBRASKA. SHE HAS FOUR CHILDREN
AND FOUR GRANDCHILDREN.

✳ *Brown Streusel Coffee Cake* ✳

ROSEMARY COWAN

2 cups brown sugar
2 cups flour
1 cup margarine, or 1 scant cup lard
1 teaspoon cinnamon
1 teaspoon baking soda
1 cup buttermilk or coffee
1 egg
1 teaspoon vanilla

Preheat oven to 375°F. Mix first four ingredients and set aside 1 cup of the mixture for streusel topping.

Mix the baking soda into the buttermilk. Add the buttermilk, egg, and vanilla to the remainder of the first mixture. Pour into a buttered 13 × 9-inch pan and sprinkle with the set-aside streusel topping.

Bake for 35 to 40 minutes.

Note: I have never used the lard called for in the original recipe, but I do use coffee instead of buttermilk. Sometimes even a cup of leftover flavored coffee.

✳

This is an old Milwaukee recipe, passed down from my grandmother, who was born in 1855. My eighty-eight-year-old mother still makes this much-loved Brown Streusel Coffee Cake for every family reunion and get-together. It is always eaten to the last crumb. Even her adult grandchildren are not above fighting over who gets the last piece. In the early 1950s, my parents had a boardinghouse for college students in Milwaukee. This coffee cake was a Sunday after-church favorite. While I was raising my children, it became our anytime treat—also a sure seller at church and school bake sales. Now that I have seven grandchildren, it's become a favorite for a new generation of hungry children. In spite of the raves that this cake always receives, it's very quick and easy to prepare, and it would be selfish not to share.

Rosemary Cowan

WAS BORN ON SEPTEMBER 15, 1934, IN MILWAUKEE, WISCONSIN. SHE HAS SEVEN CHILDREN AND SEVEN GRANDCHILDREN.

✳ *Gloria's Pound Cake* ✳

MARY DOMZALSKI

1 pound butter or margarine
   (at room temperature)
1 pound confectioners' sugar
6 eggs
1½ teaspoons vanilla extract
3 cups cake flour, sifted

TOPPINGS:
Confectioners' sugar
Fresh fruit, optional
Whipped cream, optional

Preheat oven to 325°F. Grease a 10-inch
tube pan lightly and line the bottom with wax
paper.

Cream the butter until it is light and fluffy.
Add the sugar; cream until well blended. Add
the eggs, one at a time; beat each into the batter for one minute. Stir in the vanilla. Add the
flour and blend.

Pour into the prepared tube pan. Bake for
1 hour and 20 minutes.

Cool in pan for 5 minutes, then remove
from pan and let stand on cake rack until
cold. Sprinkle with sifted confectioners' sugar
or serve sugared with assorted fresh fruits and
whipped cream.

✳

When I was a newlywed, thirty-five years ago, I asked my mother-in-law for this delicious cake recipe. She lived to be ninety years old and I am now sixty-eight, so you can be sure that we have been eating this cake for a long time and it always turns out great. It's a special recipe because it's one of just a very few my mother-in-law gave me.

Mary Domzalski

WAS BORN ON DECEMBER 22, 1926, IN CHICAGO, ILLINOIS. SHE HAS FOUR CHILDREN AND ONE GRANDCHILD.

Poverty Cake

MARY RIGSBY

1 cup water
1 cup brown sugar
2 cups raisins
⅓ cup lard (butter may be substituted)
¼ teaspoon cloves
½ teaspoon salt
1 teaspoon cinnamon
1 teaspoon nutmeg
2½ cups flour
2 teaspoons baking powder
1 teaspoon baking soda dissolved in
   1 cup water
1 teaspoon vanilla

Preheat oven to 350°F. Mix the following ingredients together and boil for three minutes: the water, brown sugar, raisins, lard, cloves, salt, cinnamon, and nutmeg. Remove from heat. When the mixture is cool, stir in the flour, baking powder, baking soda in water, and vanilla.

Grease and flour a 9-inch square pan and pour the batter into it. Bake for 30 to 40 minutes. Can also be baked in layers.

*M*y mother made up this recipe during the Depression. She called it Poverty Cake because there was so much poverty around us, so many breadlines. Sugar was scarce in those days, but with five children, my mother managed to get enough sugar. At that time, they didn't talk up cholesterol, so we just used lard. I copied it out of her cookbook and have been making it all these years.

Mary Rigsby

WAS BORN ON SEPTEMBER 10, 1917, IN LOS ANGELES, CALIFORNIA. SHE HAS THREE CHILDREN, TWO GRANDCHILDREN, AND THREE GREAT-GRANDCHILDREN.

✳ *Salted Peanut Cake* ✳

CLEO LATIMER

1 cup sugar
⅓ cup shortening
1 egg
1 cup sour milk (see note) or buttermilk
1½ cups flour
1 teaspoon baking soda
1½ cups ground salted peanuts, divided
2 teaspoons butter
1½ cups confectioners' sugar
½ teaspoon vanilla extract
3 tablespoons milk

Preheat oven to 350°F. Cream the sugar and shortening in a bowl. Add the egg, sour milk, flour, baking soda, and 1 cup of the peanuts; mix well. Pour into 2 prepared 8-inch cake pans. Bake 30 minutes. Turn out of pans and allow to cool.

Combine the butter, confectioners' sugar, vanilla, 3 tablespoons of milk, and the remaining ½ cup peanuts in a bowl; mix well. Spread between the layers and over the top of cake.

Yield: 9 servings

Note: To sour milk, place 1 teaspoon lemon juice or vinegar in a 1-cup measure and fill with milk to make 1 cup.

*S*alted Peanut Cake has always been a family favorite. My mother made this cake many times during the Depression years. It was usually the cake of choice at our family birthday dinners.

Cleo Latimer

WAS BORN ON MAY 29, 1920, IN ABERDEEN, SOUTH DAKOTA. SHE HAS FIVE CHILDREN AND SIX GRANDCHILDREN.

✳ *Irish Apple Cake* ✳

MARYAN WORK

3 cups sifted flour
¾ cup sugar
½ teaspoon salt
Grated rind of 1 lemon
2 sticks (1 cup) butter
3 egg yolks
1¾ cups, or more, chunky applesauce
½ teaspoon cinnamon
¼ teaspoon cloves

Preheat oven to 350°F. Mix the flour, sugar, salt, and lemon rind. Rub in the butter; a pastry blender is helpful for this. Add egg yolks, which are mixed in most easily with the fingertips. Put three quarters of the dough into a 13 × 9-inch pan. Press the dough into the bottom and up the sides about an inch, avoiding the corners.

Combine the other ingredients and spread this mixture on the dough in the pan. Sprinkle crumbs of the remaining dough on top.

Bake for 40 to 45 minutes.

Serve warm or cold with milk or cream. Keeps nicely.

Note: A glass pan continues to bake the bottom after removal from the oven.

My first hobby is baking. This recipe is special to us. When family members enter the house, they exclaim, "You're making Irish Apple Cake!" A hint I would give to every cook: Share the purchase of spices. Their freshness is a prime factor in the success of a dish.

Maryan Work

WAS BORN ON JUNE 15, 1916, IN PITTSBURGH, PENNSYLVANIA. SHE HAS FOUR CHILDREN, FIVE GRANDCHILDREN, AND THREE GREAT-GRANDCHILDREN.

✳ *Aunt Stella's Seven-Day Prune Cake* ✳

VICTORIA RACHEL LEVIN

1½ cups pitted prunes
¾ cup boiling coffee
1½ cups granulated sugar
¾ cup shortening (do not use butter)
3 eggs, beaten
1½ teaspoons soda
2¾ cups flour
½ teaspoon salt
2 teaspoons cinnamon
Maple Buttercream Frosting

Preheat oven to 375°F. Poach the prunes in the coffee for 15 minutes; drain (reserving coffee), and purée coarsely.

Cream together the sugar and shortening, add the beaten eggs, and mix. Add the prunes and mix well. Add the reserved coffee, in which the soda has been dissolved. Beat well. Sift together flour, salt, and cinnamon and add to batter. Beat until well combined.

Pour into 3 well-greased layer cake pans and bake for 25 minutes. Remove cakes from pans and cool completely. Put layers together with maple buttercream. This cake gathers moisture and gets better and better the longer it sits at room temperature.

MAPLE BUTTERCREAM FROSTING
½ cup Crisco
½ cup butter, softened
4 cups powdered sugar (about 1 pound)
1 teaspoon vanilla extract
2 tablespoons milk
2 teaspoons mapleine

With an electric mixture on medium speed, cream Crisco and butter. Add sugar slowly, beating until blended. Add milk, vanilla, and mapleine, raise speed to high, and beat until fluffy. Makes enough to fill and frost 1 cake.

✳

Victoria Rachel Levin

**WAS BORN IN PARIS ON
SEPTEMBER 4, 1913. SHE HAS TWO
CHILDREN, SIX GRANDCHILDREN, AND ONE
GREAT-GRANDDAUGHTER.**

I was born in France in 1913. My father took my three sisters, my mother, and me along as he sold "merchandise" (fabrics, linens, table-cloths) in Spain and France. We moved to Chicago in 1921 and stayed with my aunt Stella and her family. I married in 1932 and moved to L.A. in 1947. When my son was six years old, Aunt Stella gave me her recipe for prune cake. She told me it lasts seven days at room temperature and gets moister and moister. We've never actually experienced this, because it gets eaten right away.

✳ *Grandma Pheney's Passover Sponge Cake* ✳

LOIS HALPER

10 jumbo eggs, separated
1½ cups sugar
4 tablespoons frozen orange juice
    concentrate, defrosted
1 tablespoon lemon juice
¾ cup packed matzo cake meal (see note)
1 tablespoon potato starch, packed
    (see note)

Preheat oven to 325°F. Beat the egg yolks and sugar for 7 minutes, until light. Add the orange and lemon juices. Beat slowly with electric mixer until blended. In a separate bowl, combine the matzo cake meal and potato starch; fold into yolk mix (by hand) or slightly beat on low speed of mixer.

Beat the egg whites in a separate bowl until stiff but not dry. Fold into the yolk mix. (To make folding easier: add one quarter of the beaten whites to the yolk mix to lighten, then fold in the rest of the egg whites.)

Use an ungreased 10-inch angel food cake pan. Bake for 1 hour to 1 hour and 15 minutes. Test with a toothpick. Cool upside down. Slide knife gently around the pan to release cake after it has cooled completely. Use serrated knife to slice.

Note: All ingredients must be at room temperature.

Matzo cake meal and potato starch are available in the ethnic food aisle of most supermarkets. I buy extra boxes of matzo cake meal and potato starch during Passover week to keep in the freezer.

✳

This is a recipe that my mother gave to me, that she made during Passover holidays in the spring. Mom had tried many of the sponge cake recipes, and when frozen orange juice came on the market, she tried this cake and found it was her favorite and mine too.

When I was growing up, Passover was very special. I loved all the food served at this time, which was different from meals served the rest of the year. There were restrictions for religious reasons, and one had to improvise. Mama always felt hot cereal had to be eaten no matter what the season. We couldn't possibly survive the day. During Passover, cereal was forbidden food. Yikes! One of the breakfasts served was this sponge cake. There were many ways to change it during the day for other meals. Rhubarb sauce or strawberries were poured over. Applesauce could also be used.

My children and grandchildren still enjoy this cake, and I even use this recipe throughout the year. It is a very high and light cake. This cake looks great on a pedestal cake plate with a dusting of confectioners' sugar.

Lois Halper

WAS BORN ON FEBRUARY 13, 1930, IN PORT CHESTER, NEW YORK. SHE HAS THREE CHILDREN AND SIX GRANDCHILDREN.

✳ *Johnny Cake* ✳

HELEN J. MATTESON

2 cups flour
3 teaspoons baking powder
¾ teaspoon salt
1 cup sugar
1 cup yellow cornmeal
2 eggs, beaten
1 teaspoon vanilla
1 cup milk
½ cup margarine, melted

Preheat oven to 350°F. Mix the flour, baking powder, salt, sugar, and cornmeal. Add the beaten eggs, vanilla, and milk, then the melted margarine.

Bake in a greased loaf pan (9 × 5 inches) for 45 minutes, or bake in 12 greased muffin cups for 25 to 30 minutes.

My grandmother was born in Brooklyn, New York, in 1867. Like most cooks of her time, she kept her recipes in her head. I had to take the vague directions she gave me and put them into a modern form. This Johnny Cake is special because it is unique, not a corn bread but deliciously different. It's great toasted.

Helen J. Matteson

WAS BORN ON JUNE 3, 1914, IN
NEW YORK CITY. SHE HAS
THREE CHILDREN AND SEVEN
GRANDCHILDREN.

Orange Bread *

ELAINE M. CALDWELL

½ cup butter
1½ cups sugar
2 eggs
2¾ cups flour
2 teaspoons baking soda
1 cup buttermilk
1 cup chopped dates
1 cup chopped nuts
Juice and rind of 2 oranges

TOPPING:
Juice of 1 orange
¾ cup sugar

Preheat oven to 350°F. Combine topping ingredients and set aside. Grind dates and orange rind together in a food processor.

Mix all ingredients in the order given, beating well after each addition. Pour into a greased and lightly floured angel food cake pan.

Bake for about 40 minutes. As bread begins to brown, pour topping mixture carefully on top of bread and allow to continue baking until browned and set.

This recipe came from The Caldwell Tearoom in Corpus Christi, Texas. This quaint little tearoom was run by sisters, "Miss Julia" and "Miss Sara" Caldwell, during the 1930s. Their recipe came to me via my mother-in-law, Belle Caldwell, who had enjoyed it in Corpus Christi and served it to us in her home in Houston, where we ate Sunday dinner as a family every week from 1960 to 1996. Only the best came out of her kitchen, and this was one of her favorites.

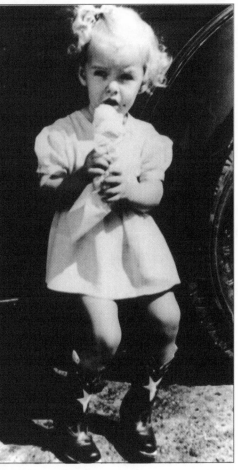

Elaine M. Caldwell

WAS BORN ON DECEMBER 15, 1937,
IN HOUSTON, TEXAS. SHE HAS
THREE CHILDREN AND TWO
GRANDCHILDREN.

✱ Grandma's Dutch Butter Cookies ✱

MARGARET CHEVALLIER

2 ounces (½ stick) margarine
2 ounces (½ stick) butter
2 tablespoons Crisco
¾ cup sugar
1 teaspoon vanilla extract
1¼ cups flour
¼ teaspoon baking soda

First, take the margarine and the real butter (softened to room temperature—don't use the microwave) and place into a bowl. Next, add the Crisco shortening and beat together with a fork. Add the ¾ cup sugar (actually, the original recipe calls for 1 full cup, but I like this lower-calorie version) to the butter mix. Also add the vanilla, and mix with a fork.

Next comes the flour. Add the flour very slowly (a spoonful at a time) while mixing with a fork. A sifter would work well. At this time, add the baking soda. Mix everything well with that same fork. Dough should be kind of sticky yet kind of crumbly.

Turn the oven on to preheat to 325°F. before you get your hands greasy from rolling the dough balls.

Now it's time to roll the dough into little balls. These should be a little smaller than a Ping-Pong ball, but bigger than a marble.

Place these on a regular cookie sheet, not the nonstick kind. Don't spray anything on the cookie sheet.

Next, mash down the little cookie balls with a fork. This should be done at right angles to each other. To avoid having the dough stick to the fork, you may want to dip the fork into some water. Cookies should be around ¼ inch high after mashing. Round up any splits in the cookies with your fingers.

Bake for 20 minutes. Cookies should be a tiny bit light brown around the edges. Some may get done earlier than others, therefore it may be necessary to take a few out from the edge of the cookie sheet, and then put the rest back in for a minute or two. Place them on a paper bag or fancy plate to cool, and then store in one of those cookie tins with two paper towels in the bottom.

Yield: about 2½ dozen cookies

I usually make these cookies without a recipe, but one of my grandsons has now put it in column form so that others might be able to share in it. Never make a double recipe or else the cookies won't turn out right. It is best to get all of the ingredients out onto the counter before you start, and put them away one by one as you use them. This way, you won't forget to put anything in, and you won't have a big mess to put away when you're finished.

This recipe comes from my mother, who, along with her Dutch friends, made them often back in Holland. As a mother, grandmother, and great-grandmother, I always had these cookies on hand, and my grandchildren tell me I would dole them out as if they were pieces of gold. Just one of these melt-in-your-mouth treats would send my grandchildren bragging that they had the best grandma in the world.

Margaret Chevallier

WAS BORN ON MARCH 5, 1905, IN LISSE, NEBRASKA. SHE HAS SEVEN CHILDREN, TWENTY-NINE GRANDCHILDREN, AND TWENTY-SEVEN GREAT-GRANDCHILDREN.

✷ *Dina's Mandel Broyt* (Jewish Biscotti) ✷

DINA ROSEN

½ cup less 1 tablespoon oil (canola/corn oil
    blend is recommended)

3 eggs

1 cup sugar

1¼ teaspoon baking powder

½ teaspoon vanilla

1 cup chopped nuts (walnuts, cashews,
    macadamia, or pistachio are most highly
    recommended. Even though *mandel*
    means "almond" in Yiddish, I do not
    favor this nut.)

2½–3 cups flour

In a large bowl, combine the oil, eggs, and
sugar. Beat with electric mixer until well
blended. Add baking powder and vanilla and
continue beating until well mixed. Add the
nuts and mix with a large spoon. Sift the flour
directly into the bowl and continue mixing
with spoon until well blended.

Refrigerate at least 1 hour to overnight, de-
pending on your schedule. Preheat oven to
325°F. Divide dough into thirds and put on a
large ungreased cookie sheet in three "strips"
of approximately 2″ × 14″ lengths, at least 3″
apart.

Bake for ½ hour or until bottom is golden
brown. Let cool 5–10 minutes. Cut strips
crosswise into ¾″ pieces (there will be approximately 16–18 pieces per strip). Keep
the end pieces slightly wider—they are the
tastiest.

Turn oven temperature up to 350°F and
return pieces to cookie sheet with the cut
sides facing up and down. Bake for 20 more
minutes or until golden brown on bottom.

Let cool. *Mandel Broyt* can be refrigerated
or frozen. Store in airtight bags or jars.

✷

started cooking when I was six. There were eight children and my father was very religious — he didn't work; he prayed all day. We were very poor, so my mother brought in what she could. She was the breadwinner and the breadmaker. But even at that age, when I made my first potato latke, I never followed her recipes. I did everything on my own.

I still do. I cook a five-course dinner for the kids every Wednesday. Between shopping in Fairfax and preparing the meal — it takes me two full days. Sometimes — "khob nisht kayn koyes" — I have no strength. But I have to keep going. What else can I do at my age? Cooking gives me joy, makes me feel useful. I must be doing something right because even with all the busy schedules, they still come. And no matter what's on the table that week, the last course is always tea . . . and Mandel Broyt.

Dina Rosen
(standing)

WAS BORN ON MAY 6, 1909, IN FRYSZTAK, POLAND. SHE HAS ONE CHILD, THREE GRANDCHILDREN, AND THREE GREAT-GRANDCHILDREN.

✳ *Sinkers* ✳

VIRGINIA SYRYLO

FOR THE COOKIES:

1 cup butter or margarine

2 cups sugar

4 eggs

1 teaspoon vanilla extract

1 teaspoon butternut flavoring
    or ½ teaspoon almond extract

1 teaspoon baking soda

1 teaspoon baking powder

4½ cups flour

FOR THE GLAZE:

2 cups confectioners' sugar

2 tablespoons hot water

    Cream together the butter and sugar. Add the eggs, then the vanilla extract, butternut or almond flavoring, baking soda, baking powder, and flour until a soft dough forms. (Sometimes you may need more or less of the flour.) Chill the dough until it is firm enough to roll.

    Preheat oven to 350°F. Roll out the dough to ¼ inch thick and cut out with any seasonal cookie cutter. Place the cookies on a greased cookie sheet. Bake for about 12 minutes, or until light brown.

    Just before the cookies are done, combine the confectioners' sugar and hot water for the glaze. Remove the cookies from the oven and brush glaze over them while still hot. The glaze will become hard and shiny.

    Yield: about 3 dozen

✳

Virginia Syrylo

WAS BORN ON SEPTEMBER 26, 1930, IN DU BOIS, PENNSYLVANIA. SHE HAS THREE CHILDREN AND TWO GRANDCHILDREN.

When I was a little girl and money was tight, during the Depression years, my mother made cookies we called "Sinkers." She made these cookies for Christmas and holidays and special occasions. We would kid her and say, "When we put the cookie in a glass of milk it would sink to the bottom"—hence the name. We loved those cookies, and my children and grandchildren love them as much as we did.

✻ *Grandma's Oatmeal Cookies* ✻

HARRIET AXELRAD

$1\frac{1}{4}$ cups sugar
$\frac{1}{2}$ cup shortening
2 eggs
6 tablespoons molasses
$1\frac{3}{4}$ cups flour
1 teaspoon baking soda
1 teaspoon salt
$\frac{3}{4}$ teaspoon cinnamon
2 cups quick-cooking rolled oats
$\frac{1}{2}$ cup chopped nuts
1 cup seedless raisins

Preheat oven to 375°F. Cream together the sugar, shortening, and eggs. Add the molasses. Gradually add the dry ingredients, nuts, and raisins.

Drop by teaspoonfuls onto a greased cookie sheet. Bake for 8 to 10 minutes—not until dry inside.

M y grandmother worked in a bakery shop in New York in the 1880s. She gave this recipe to her children. What makes it special is that the cookies are soft, due to the molasses. Growing up, my children liked the cookies, so I had to find hiding places for them. Usually they found them. Once I hid them in the washing machine.

Harriet Axelrad

WAS BORN ON JANUARY 27, 1916, IN
KANSAS CITY, MISSOURI. SHE HAS FIVE
CHILDREN AND EIGHT GRANDCHILDREN.

✳ *Oat Macaroons* ✳

JAN CLAUSSEN

6 ounces shortening

2 ounces butter

1 cup brown sugar

1 cup granulated sugar

2 eggs

1 cup shredded coconut

1¼ cups flour

3 cups quick-cooking rolled oats

1 teaspoon baking soda

½ teaspoon vanilla extract

¾ teaspoon salt

Preheat oven to 350°F. Cream the fat and sugars. Add the eggs; beat. Stir in the other ingredients. Drop from a teaspoon onto a cookie sheet. Bake for 12 to 15 minutes. They are the best!

This recipe came into my hand, literally, in a rather unusual way. Years ago, when my husband and I were newlyweds, we visited his parents often. After we exchanged greetings, I always made a beeline for the cookie jar, hoping my mother-in-law, Leona Claussen, had baked my favorites. One visit, I stuck my hand in the jar and found only a 3 x 5-inch card with her recipe. She grinned and said, "I can't keep up. It's time you made them for yourself." At the time she wasn't a grandmother yet. She's gone now and missed mightily. Neither of my husband's parents got to meet their great-grandson. His grandmother (me) plans to bake his first batch next week.

Jan Claussen

WAS BORN ON MARCH 24, 1932, IN PITTSBURGH, PENNSYLVANIA. SHE HAS TWO CHILDREN AND ONE GRANDCHILD.

✳ *Evie's Jingle Bell Cookies* ✳

CATHERINE SCHEIBE

3 cups flour
1 teaspoon baking soda
1 teaspoon cinnamon
Pinch of salt
1 pound butter
1½ cups sugar
2 eggs, lightly beaten
1 teaspoon vanilla extract
½ pound green candied cherries
½ pound red candied cherries
1½ pounds diced dates
1 cup chopped walnuts
1 cup filberts
1 cup broken pecans

Sift together 2½ cups flour, the baking soda, cinnamon, and salt. In a separate, large mixing bowl, cream together the butter and sugar. Add the eggs and vanilla. In half-cup increments, incorporate the flour mixture. Toss the chopped dates in the remaining one half of flour to keep the pieces from clinging together, then add all the fruits and nuts to the dough.

Drop small amounts (about 1-inch diameter) onto a greased cookie sheet and bake each batch for 20 minutes in a preheated 325°F oven. Keep a close eye on each batch, as the cookies should be light golden brown, and not dark. Cool on cookie racks.

✳

*A*untie Evie *(right) never had any children, so her nieces and nephews were often enlisted at holiday time to help with the cookie baking. She was patient with us and didn't scold us if we sampled the cookie dough. I remember her showing me how to make a fancy pressed sugar cookie, using the bottom of a cut-glass tumbler.*

This tradition of cookie baking and sharing continued after I grew up, married, and moved to a farm in North Dakota. When our children were small, Auntie Evie shared her "Jingle Bell" cookies with us and they became one of our favorites. They are easy to make and look pretty on the cookie plate. The only trick is to make sure each cookie has a sample of each nut and fruit while keeping them small. Jingle Bells resemble fruitcake in appearance only. They have a delicious cookie crunch and flavor all their own.

Catherine Scheibe
(seated, at left)

WAS BORN ON MAY 22, 1940, IN
ST. PAUL, MINNESOTA. SHE HAS
FOUR CHILDREN AND ONE
GRANDDAUGHTER.

✳ *Raisin Cookies* ✳

ESTHER ZIMMERMAN

FOR THE COOKIE DOUGH:

2 cups sugar

½ cup (scant) butter

2 eggs

5 cups flour

1 cup milk

1 teaspoon soda

2 teaspoons baking powder

FOR THE FILLING:

1 cup ground raisins

½ cup water

1 cup sugar

1½ tablespoons flour

Mix the ingredients for the dough together in the order given. Set aside in a cool place or in the refrigerator.

Boil the ingredients for the filling together until thick, about 10 minutes. Cool to room temperature.

Preheat oven to 350°F. Shape the cookie dough into balls and thumbprint each one. Place some filling in the hole and put a little dough on the top to cover filling.

Bake 15 to 20 minutes until golden brown.

✳

This recipe is from an old friend who baked these cookies until she was ninety years old. Drop the dough and put a thumbprint on it. It's a soft cookie and those are usually the ones I like.

Esther Zimmerman

WAS BORN ON JUNE 5, 1923, IN EFFORTA, PENNSYLVANIA. SHE HAS THIRTEEN CHILDREN AND NINETY GRANDCHILDREN.

✳ *Brownies* ✳

GERI L. THAYER

1 cup butter
4 squares bakers' bitter chocolate
4 eggs, beaten lightly
2 cups sugar
1 cup flour plus additional for pan
1 teaspoon vanilla extract

Preheat oven to 350°F. Grease and flour (or use Pam) a 13 × 9-inch pan.

Melt together the butter and chocolate. In a separate bowl, combine the eggs, sugar, flour, and vanilla. Stir the chocolate mixture into the egg mixture and mix well.

Bake for 15 minutes *or less*. The secret is not to let the brownies cook through. The top will have a slight crust, but the knife should come out with batter on it. If they are too runny to cut, just put them in the refrigerator to harden for a while and serve them cold. A friend in New York City doubles the recipe and uses the same size pan, and they come out thicker.

Note: When this recipe was made, raw eggs weren't considered a danger.

I was raised in Chicago, Illinois, in an upper-middle-class family where both parents were professional people and worked every day. We had a maid and a cook, and I was "not allowed" in the kitchen. I was about ten years old when, on the cook's day off, the maid taught me to make brownies.

When I was fourteen years old my family moved to a brownstone house on the Near North Side of Chicago. The movers had finished for the day but had left many empty cartons piled high in front of the house. My mother was at home and everyone was busy unpacking, so I went to the kitchen and baked brownies. While they were cooling, the maid saw flames from the third-story window and yelled, "FIRE." My mother said that we should all take our most important valuables with us and get out quickly. The fire department came and extinguished the blaze while we were all standing in the street. We must have been quite a sight: My mother was holding on to her huge jewelry box, the maid had her rosary and crucifix that had been blessed by the Pope, the cook had pictures of her family in Sweden, and I had the brownies.

Geri L. Thayer

WAS BORN ON MAY 2, 1938, IN CHICAGO, ILLINOIS. SHE HAS SEVEN CHILDREN (INCLUDING THREE STEPCHILDREN) AND EIGHT GRANDCHILDREN.

✳ *Chocolate Cake-like Brownies* ✳

JIMMIE R. JACOBS

FOR THE BROWNIES:

2 cups sifted flour
2 cups sugar
½ teaspoon salt
2 sticks margarine
1 cup water
4 tablespoons dark cocoa
2 eggs
½ cup buttermilk
1 teaspoon vanilla extract
1 teaspoon baking soda

FOR THE ICING:

1 stick margarine
4 tablespoons cocoa
6 tablespoons milk
1 box confectioners' sugar, sifted
½ cup chopped nuts
1 teaspoon vanilla extract

Preheat oven to 350°F. Sift the flour, measure, and resift twice with the sugar and salt. Set aside.

Bring the margarine, water, and cocoa to a boil and remove from heat. Stir until the margarine has melted. Pour into the flour mixture. Beat until smooth.

Beat the eggs well. Add the buttermilk, vanilla, and baking soda. Pour at once into the cocoa mixture. Mix this batter well and pour into a greased, floured pan (jelly roll size — 17 × 11 inches).

Bake for 20 minutes, or until done.

Five minutes before the cake is done, make the icing: Mix the margarine, cocoa, and milk. Heat over flame (don't boil), stirring until mixed well.

Stir in the confectioners' sugar, nuts, and vanilla until smooth. Pour over the hot cake. Cool and cut.

✳

I raised my three children on this recipe. Of course, back in the forties and fifties there was not much ado over calories and allergies. When I look back I get a sense of freedom and place where time and space are one. The choice to indulge was an individual choice, and the whole family chose to encourage me in whatever I cooked—especially the Chocolate Cake-like Brownies.

Jimmie R. Jacobs

WAS BORN ON MAY 3, 1922, IN BOLIVAR COUNTY, MISSISSIPPI. SHE HAS THREE CHILDREN AND SEVEN GRANDCHILDREN.

✱ *Citrus Phyllo Baskets* ✱

ANTOINETTE COX

FOR THE PHYLLO SHELLS:

4 sheets phyllo dough
¼ cup melted unsalted butter
3 tablespoons finely chopped walnuts
3 tablespoons white bread crumbs, dried
Pam

FOR THE FILLING:

1 package (8 ounces) cream cheese
6 tablespoons butter or margarine
1 teaspoon vanilla extract
8 cups powdered sugar, sifted
⅓ cup fresh lemon juice
⅓ cup fresh lime juice
2 teaspoons finely shredded lemon peel
2 teaspoons finely shredded lime peel

FOR THE TOPPING:

1 or 2 fresh kiwis, sliced
Fresh sliced strawberries, or boysenberries
    or fruit of choice

To make the shells: Preheat oven to 350°F. Place one sheet of phyllo on the countertop. Brush with melted butter or margarine. Sprinkle 1 tablespoon of the chopped walnuts and 1 tablespoon of the bread crumbs on the phyllo sheet. Place a second sheet of phyllo on top of the first sheet. Butter this sheet and sprinkle with 1 tablespoon of the chopped walnuts and 1 tablespoon of the bread crumbs. Repeat with a third sheet of phyllo, sprinkling the rest of the nuts and bread crumbs over it. Top with a fourth sheet; brush with butter. Cut with a sharp knife into 12 squares, about 4 × 4 inches each.

Spray every other cup of a 12-cup muffin pan (½-cup size) with Pam. Place one phyllo square in each of the alternating sprayed cups. (You will bake 6 shells at a time.) Press the squares down into the cup to shape. The corners of the squares will stick up. Bake for about 10 minutes, or until light brown. Remove from the muffin pan; cool on a wire rack.

While the shells are baking, make the filling: In a medium bowl combine the cream cheese, the 6 tablespoons butter, and the vanilla extract and powdered sugar. Beat with an electric mixer on medium speed until fluffy. Add the lemon juice, lime juice, lemon peel, and lime peel; beat until mixture is fluffy. Refrigerate until ready to serve.

To assemble the baskets: Spoon the filling into the cooled phyllo shells. Arrange freshly sliced kiwis and strawberries or boysenberries on
✱ top of the filling.

I learned to cook by watching my mother, Rose Dittrick, and my grandmother, Barbara Dittrick, who lived on a farm in Downey, California. Both my mother and my grandmother made everything from scratch, and dinner wouldn't be complete without a bowl of soup with fresh homemade noodles in it.

My sister and I would tag along behind Grandma as she made her way through her boysenberry patch, or when she'd pick fresh peaches, deciding what she'd make for dessert. Dreams are made of fresh fruit-filled raised doughnuts, strudels, and cobblers. My mother was a great cook, and you learned by doing in her kitchen. I loved watching her hand-stretch phyllo dough over her hands and arms. You knew it wouldn't be long before you'd be smelling pumpkin or apple strudel when the dough got so thin that you'd see her arms and hands through the dough. Now I want to share special times with my granddaughters, so I will plan times to make things in the kitchen with them.

Antoinette Cox

WAS BORN ON AUGUST 30, 1939, IN HUNTINGTON PARK, CALIFORNIA. SHE HAS TWO CHILDREN AND TWO GRANDCHILDREN.

✷ *Charlotte Russe* ✷

MARY SJOGREN

1 quart heavy or whipping cream
1 pint milk
6 eggs, lightly beaten
1½ cups sugar
2 teaspoons vanilla extract
4 envelopes Knox gelatin
¼ cup cold water
2 packages ladyfingers or
    1-pound loaf sponge cake

Whip the cream to a stiff froth. Set aside.

Add the eggs to the milk. Add the sugar and vanilla. Cook mixture over hot water until it is a thick custard.

Soak the gelatin in the quarter cup cold water, and warm over hot water until dissolved. Whisk into the custard and chill. When the custard is cold, lightly beat in the whipped cream.

Line the bottom of a charlotte mold with buttered paper and line the sides with sponge cake, which has been sliced lengthwise and then crosswise ½-inch thick, or ladyfingers. Fill with the custard cream. Put in a cold place or, in summer, on ice.

To turn out, dip the mold for a moment in hot water. In draining the custard cream, all that drips through can be rewhipped.

When I was nineteen I was orphaned, and I went to live with my dad's mother, "Mama Annie." Ann Kelly Hardi was born in Jacksonville, Florida, around 1885, and lost her whole family in a yellow fever epidemic at two years of age. She was raised by the nuns till she was fifteen, then went to work as a mother's helper. Sitting in the park with her charges, she met my granddad, Dan Hardi. He was an itinerant house painter of nineteen who had run away from home at thirteen, sailed before the mast, and fought in the Spanish-American War. He and Mama Annie were married a year later. He was sheriff of Miami twice, and made and lost a million dollars twice, too. Through it all, she was a five-foot tower of strength, short and round with dark eyes and, to her death, dark hair. We used to tease her and say she was really an Irish Gypsy.

This recipe belonged to my Mama Annie. You can tell that this is a true olden-times recipe. It was written before they even had refrigerators.

Mary Sjogren

WAS BORN ON JULY 7, 1932, IN MIAMI BEACH, FLORIDA. SHE HAS FOUR CHILDREN AND FOUR GRANDCHILDREN.

Abuelita's Flan

MARIA MEDINA

6 eggs
1 can (14 ounces) sweetened
   condensed milk
1 can (12 ounces) evaporated milk
¾ cup water
2 teaspoons vanilla extract
4 tablespoons sugar

Preheat oven to 350°F. Mix the first 5 ingredients and set aside. Heat the sugar until it caramelizes. Pour the sugar onto the bottom of a 9-inch round cake pan; coat the pan and let the sugar harden. (Make sure that the sugar has not burned.) Pour in the mixture and cover. Place pan in a larger pan and fill the lower pan halfway up with hot water.

Bake for 1½ hours. Insert a toothpick to see if it is done. If the toothpick comes out clean . . . it's ready.

Cool overnight. Run a knife around the edge of the pan to loosen the flan and turn over onto a serving tray.

Maria Medina

WAS BORN MARIA MERCEDES RIVERA IN
ABONITO, PUERTO RICO, ON SEPTEMBER 25,
1926. SHE HAS FOUR CHILDREN AND
SIX GRANDCHILDREN.

M*y fondest memories are of my grand-parents, since they raised me until the age of twelve. As a child, I watched my abuelita (grandmother) prepare various dishes, often with whatever she found in the kitchen at that moment, since money was scarce. I, like most children, loved desserts, and my favorite dish was Abuelita's Flan.*

I came to the mainland from Puerto Rico when I was nineteen years old. I eventually married, and when I started cooking for my own family, I changed the recipe. I found that using evaporated and condensed milk instead of whole milk made the flan much tastier. My four children and six grandchildren agree.

✳ *Peanut Brittle* ✳

PHYLLIS VAN WAGENEN

2 cups sugar
1 cup water
1 cup corn syrup (light Karo)
$\frac{1}{4}$ teaspoon salt
1 tablespoon butter
1 teaspoon vanilla
1 teaspoon baking soda
2 cups raw Spanish peanuts

Combine water, sugar, syrup, and salt in a large heavy-bottomed saucepan. Bring to a boil without stirring and cook to 236°F on a candy thermometer (softball stage). Add peanuts. Stir constantly and continue to cook to 290°F (hard-crack stage). Remove from heat and add the butter, vanilla, and soda. Stir quickly and vigorously for 1–2 minutes until candy begins to turn opaque. Then pour onto a large buttered cookie sheet or marble slab or kitchen countertop. With the help of a metal spatula, flip the candy over upon itself. Then begin to stretch it with the spatula until candy begins to harden. Use your fingers to help, if necessary. This makes the candy thin and brittle. When candy is hard, break it into pieces and store in airtight container.

✳

I grew up on a farm in North Ogden, Utah, where my father farmed row crops, fruit, chickens, and dairy cows. I learned to cook on the farm at an early age, specializing in baking bread, rolls, cakes, and pies, but my family lines up for my fudge and peanut brittle. My grandchildren have come to appreciate the fact that Grandma is going to feed them if they come into the house. I expect all participants at a meal to clean their plates. I always say, "Better belly burst than good food spoil." However, there is never a need to twist an arm when it comes to my peanut brittle.

Though my family places cooking as my greatest skill, I think it ranks third after my offspring and my golf trophies. Since finding golf early on in college, I've won many local amateur golf tournaments, but had my first hole-in-one at the age of seventy! Amazingly, I've repeated that accomplishment on two subsequent occasions.

Phyllis Barker Van Wagenen

WAS BORN ON DECEMBER 6, 1915, IN NORTH OGDEN, UTAH. SHE HAS SIX CHILDREN, SEVENTEEN GRANDCHILDREN, AND FOUR GREAT-GRANDCHILDREN.

✳ *Sadie Mae Jackson's Bread Pudding* ✳

SADIE MAE JACKSON

3 slices (small loaf) or 2 slices (large loaf)
  good quality white bread, cubed
2 eggs
½ cup granulated sugar
1 tablespoon vanilla extract, or to taste
2 cups milk
⅓ cup raisins
⅓ cup brown sugar
1 teaspoon cinnamon

Preheat oven to 350°F. Cut the bread into ½-inch cubes. Set aside. Beat the eggs in a medium-size bowl. Add the sugar and vanilla (you can use plenty of vanilla). Set aside.

Heat the milk until little bubbles show on edge. Remove the milk from the heat and very slowly add it to the beaten eggs.

Line a baking dish (about quart size) with the cubed bread. Sprinkle the raisins over the bread cubes. Slowly pour the hot milk mixture over the bread cubes and raisins. The cubed bread will rise to the top. Sprinkle the brown sugar and cinnamon over the bread.

Set the baking dish in a pan with hot water about 1 inch deep. Bake at 350°F for 30 minutes. Then increase the heat to 400°F and continue to bake until the pudding is set (when an inserted knife comes out clean).

I was born on a farm outside Chicago and was only able to finish eighth grade, as high school was too far from home to attend. But my education in a one-room schoolhouse provided me with a lifelong interest in books and learning that resulted in my committing to memory many poems. By the time I married in 1926, at the age of eighteen, I had already developed an interest in cooking. After marriage, I canned an average of seven hundred jars a year of fruit, vegetables, jellies, and jams — nearly all the ingredients raised on our farm outside Dearborn, Michigan. During World War II, I cooked for USO servicemen, and still correspond with some of them. When our children grew up and left home, we built a lodge near Stowe, Vermont, and served meals to guests; my Bread Pudding was a constant favorite. This bread pudding is also my grandsons' favorite. It has evolved over the years from experimentation with different variations of the recipe. What makes this bread pudding special is the creation of more custard.

Sadie Mae Jackson

WAS BORN ON APRIL 5, 1908, IN CHICAGO, ILLINOIS. SHE HAS TWO CHILDREN AND TWO GRANDCHILDREN.

Lye Soap

FLO BURTNETT

1½ gallons water
3 cans (13-ounce size) lye
15 pounds cracklins or any other fat
3 tablespoons borax

Put the water into an empty wash pot. Empty 3 ten-cent (now $2.98!) cans of lye in the water. When the lye is dissolved, add the cracklins—or any other fat you may have on hand. Boil till the fat is eaten by the lye. Rake the fire back and put in the borax, and "take a see." Then, with a big stick, stir until you can't stir anymore.

Pour into pans, allow to cool down and harden, and cut into squares of soap.

This recipe, which is over a hundred years old, was given to my grandmother in 1912. Grandmother was a new bride, and her mother told her how to make lye soap. My mother, who is eighty-four, used to make it, too.

I grew up on a farm where we did everything ourselves — butchered hogs, picked wild plums and greens, canned, and made our own lye soap. We had a black kettle outside with coals and fire. We used the soap to wash the kids, wash the dishes, wash the floor. My mother would use her paring knife to chip the soap up so that it'd dissolve better in the laundry. It was the early version of Ivory Flakes.

We used lye soap till probably around 1940. I found the recipe in Grandma's things when she passed away. I always found it amusing when she would say "Take a see," which means it is time to look at the soap and see if it's ready.

Flo Burtnett

WAS BORN ON APRIL 23, 1936, IN ELK CITY, OKLAHOMA. SHE HAS TWO CHILDREN AND FIVE GRANDCHILDREN.

* Index *

❋

✳

✳

These pages are dedicated to holding the secret recipes of the grandmothers in your life.

Love Always, Grandma

✳ *Love Always, Grandma* ✳

_____

✷ *Love Always, Grandma* ✷

✳ *Love Always, Grandma* ✳

_____

ATTENTION ALL GRANDMAS!
Do you have your own treasured family
recipe that you'd like to see handed down?
Why not share it with us? Send a recipe
and, if possible, a photograph of yourself.
We just might publish it in our next book.

Send recipes to:
Mindy Marin
c/o Ballantine Books
201 East 50th Street, 23rd Floor
New York, NY 10022